Plants as Therapy

Plants as Therapy

Elvin McDonald

A FRANK E. TAYLOR BOOK

Praeger Publishers · New York

Published in the United States of America in 1976
by Praeger Publishers, Inc.
111 Fourth Avenue, New York, N.Y. 10003

Library of Congress Catalog Card Number: 74-33026
ISBN 0-275-22090-7

Printed in the United States of America

TO MY PARENTS,
who allowed
me the freedom
to grow

Acknowledgments

Plants as Therapy, more than any other book I have written, reflects my lifelong involvement with plants and the people who grow them. To all who have helped, guided, challenged, and inspired me, I am indebted.

Special thanks go to the individuals whose lifework centers on horticultural therapy, and who have shared their experiences freely: Andrew Barber, Howard D. Brooks, Alice W. Burlingame, Rhea R. McCandliss, Dr. Howard A. Rusk, and Robert Steffen.

To my family and close friends who nurtured me and the manuscript, I offer love and appreciation: Frank E. Taylor, who conceived the idea; Bill Mulligan, who guided its development; Pat Frost, who gathered information and gave me insights into therapy as well as plants from the viewpoint of a nongardener; Joanne McKay, who tirelessly typed the first draft; Arthur Leaman and the staff of the Golden Lemon in St. Kitts, British West Indies, who provided me with the perfect atmosphere in which to write the final manuscript; Mary Heathcote, who has made copy-editing a fine art; Mary Otto, who stands guard at my door and telephone to allow me the privacy I need to write; and my children, Mark, Steven, and Jeannene, who in countless ways helped me to write this book, not the least of which was to read over my shoulder from time to time, encouraging me by saying they liked what they read and on some occasions giving me a welcome neck rub.

ELVIN McDONALD

New York City
February 1976

vii

Contents

Plants as Therapy

Introduction

Although by reading *Plants as Therapy* you may learn something of what plants need to grow, this is not a book about how to grow plants but rather a book about what growing plants can do for you.

And what do plants do for us besides give us oxygen to breathe and provide shelter, food, and clothing? Scientists have expended great efforts establishing what they believe to be our minimum daily nutrient requirements, but they have not yet determined our minimum daily nature requirements, the time we need to spend in the presence of living plants.

Gardeners have always known that plants can provide emotional sustenance. For some two hundred years people concerned with mental health have recognized the therapeutic value of plants. Now so many people are turning to plants as a pastime, and the intensity of interest is so great, that the question must be asked: What is our minimum daily requirement for association with plants?

Scientists may never have the answer to this question, but I believe that plants have enormous potential for maintaining emotional stability and actually improving the lives of human beings. To support my belief, I can offer not only my own experiences and those of other gardeners but documented evidence from professional therapists, who in increasing numbers are turning to plants for the treatment of the physically and emotionally handicapped.

I have written this book from two vantage points. First, I have been actively and intensely involved with plants since I was a small child and have made a career of writing and lecturing about how to grow them. Second, I am a thirty-nine-year-old city dweller who suffers the stresses and anxieties common to every individual in today's society.

My lifelong relationship with plants began when, as a three-year-old, I transplanted a bean sprout from my mother's garden and it grew all winter in our kitchen window. When I was nine I built my first greenhouse. When I was fourteen I founded a national society for the gloxinia, my favorite flower. When I was nineteen I helped found *Flower and Garden* magazine. I wrote the *World Book of House Plants,* became garden editor of *House Beautiful* magazine, helped create *Popular Gardening Indoors* for CBS, and have the happiest life with my children and family of anyone I know. However charmed my life may seem, it is rooted in hard and valuable growing experiences.

I was born in the western Oklahoma Panhandle, the heart of the Dust Bowl, near the end of the Great Depression. Until my high school days, when oil was discovered on that dry land, my parents and I had very little money. To buy a hundred-dollar upright so I could learn to play the piano meant that they did without something important.

Except in an occasional rainy season, the Oklahoma Panhandle is lonely, isolated, barren country. Growing flowers there took a herculean effort on my part, and besides, it was not the sort of thing boys in that part of the world were supposed to do. I chose to study opera in college rather than horticulture or journalism. I married young, became a father young, failed in my own business young.

Then I picked up the pieces of my professional life, and in my personal life became a divorced man. Now there's alimony and child support, private schools and orthodontia. Like most city folk I am surrounded by insidious grime and crime. There's noise stress and air pollution and rotten politics, and New York, which is now my hometown, is on the brink of bankruptcy. My planes get caught in hold patterns, some of my plants get sick, and the children don't always pick up after themselves. I have to cope with office politics and wonder if I can afford the supermarket checkout, then walk home along streets littered with debris. I work hard a lot, I play hard less than I would like. It's not easy to make ends meet, to work against deadlines, and to keep calm.

But I am calm most of the time, thanks to my day-to-day involvement with plants. Sometimes all I need to feel peaceful is to touch a velvety petal or furry leaf or to remove the withered flowers from the African violets. At other times I relieve my anxieties by losing myself in an all-out potting, grooming, feeding, and watering session with my plants.

Plants work for me. And they are working for thousands of other people whose stories form the basis for this book. We have elected to pursue an alternative way of coping with life. Take a pill if you will, but we say, "Take a plant."

1 ❧ Beginnings

My parents met and married in Texas, but shortly thereafter they borrowed the money to buy several hundred acres of
land to the north, an act that was to make them Oklahomans
for life. Unfortunately, 1929 hit two years later, and they were
at the beginning of what was to be a seven-year drought. Spring
after spring the buffalo-grass pasture showed less and less green
as fierce winds stirred up the dry topsoil and turned it into boil-
ing clouds of dust. The wind blew with such force that house-
wives in Illinois complained of having Oklahoma dust on their
furniture.

Every spring my mother and father had to scrape together
enough money to buy seeds and tractor fuel to put in summer
row crops. It was the same struggle in September, at wheat-
planting time. One crop barely paid for the next. What my
parents ate they grew from the land. What the land could not
produce they went without, in the little two-room clapboard
house that stood halfway up a hill, fully exposed to the winds.

My mother cooked with kerosene in the kitchen, and in the other room there was a potbellied coal stove.

Into this barren time and place I was born at four in the morning in February 1937. "A terrible dust storm began about one hour after Elvin arrived," Mother wrote in my baby book. "We had to have lamplight until eleven o'clock." In later years she always said that I brought the last of the dreadful dust storms of the thirties, and whether or not this was actually so I never questioned, because my parents kept from me their worries about whether or not we were going to have food, clothing, and shelter. I liked the cereal my mother made by roasting and grinding some of the grain sorghum that we raised for the chickens. I liked wearing my cousins' hand-me-downs. And I thought it was exciting to bundle up in the winter and have my father hoist me over his shoulder for our nightly dash to the unheated dugout behind the house, where we slept.

From my first summer, when Mother carried me in a basket to where she gathered vegetables in the garden or hoed weeds in the truck patch, I existed in a brown environment struggling to be green. My earliest memory of this life dates to the autumn of 1940, when I was three and a half years old. It was a crisp, clear October day and Mother knew that a killing frost was on its way. As she picked the last of the green tomatoes to make a piccalilli, I wandered around the vegetable garden feeling sad that Jack Frost was about to ruin what had been my summer playground.

Then I discovered a bean sprout and asked my mother if I could grow it in the house. Although she generally encouraged my games, this time she said no, beans were not house plants, and besides, they couldn't be transplanted. Rebellion. Of course I could transplant it to a tin can of soil and make it grow. I insisted, and that is exactly what happened. The bean plant grew all winter in a sunny window, up one side, across the top, and back down the other.

The amazing thing about what happened with the bean plant that fall and winter is that although my mother was technically right, plants are unpredictable. No gardener to the trowel born would ever think of transplanting a bean seedling or growing it indoors in winter. When Mother saw that I was going to dig up the bean, she wisely chose to consider that I was defying nature and not her. Rather than ignore or scold me, she put down her work and took the time to show me how to transplant a seedling growing in the open garden to a container of soil. She then explained that if the transplant was to live, I would have to take the responsibility of watering it often enough so that the soil would always feel moist when I pinched some of it between my fingers, and never let it get dry enough to make the leaves wilt. I also remember quite clearly that she told me the best place in the house for the bean plant would be in the kitchen, which was warm and, because it faced the west, had the most sunlight.

From the time it was transplanted, the seedling grew like Jack's beanstalk. My parents both took as much pleasure in it as I did. Although they came from generations of farm folk, neither of them had ever isolated a single plant and watched it develop. They thought only in terms of a long row of tomatoes, a patch of corn, or several hundred acres of wheat. The bean gave them a new sense of themselves as growers while it was teaching me the beginning essentials of container gardening. No matter how much it rained or snowed outdoors, I still had to water the bean often enough to keep the soil moist. And I could see that the leaves wanted to be in the sun because the stems always reached toward the window, not into the room.

Three-year-olds of my generation did not have a busy schedule of watching television and going to nursery school, so I had plenty of time to take care of my bean plant. Only once, the week after Christmas, did I forget to water it. I discovered the drooping leaves at suppertime, and immediately gave the bean a big drink of water. My parents reassured me that it would soon perk up, but I undressed for bed as soon as we finished eating, wrapped myself in my patchwork quilt, and sat on the floor, waiting and watching in the moonlight just to be sure everything was going to be all right. Of course I woke up the next morning in my own bed in the dugout, but when I ran to the kitchen and looked, the plant was as leafy and green as before.

A few days later I saw that some of the older leaves were turning yellow and sickly looking, and some of the baby leaves seemed to have dried up. My father showed me how to cut off what seemed to be dead and explained that this was called pruning, the same thing he did in early spring to the fruit trees in the orchard in front of our house. He also cautioned that if I ever forgot to water the bean again it might not recover.

By my fourth spring I was always out with my parents when they were planting seeds. Both did a lot of planting, Mother the vegetable garden and Father the larger truck patch as well as the fields of grain sorghum. Mother sowed by hand, but Father pulled a drill or other mechanical seeding equipment behind his tractor. Both of them seemed to know instinctively when to plant what, how far apart to make the rows, how far apart in the rows to space the seeds, and how deep to plant them. They too had grown up in the footsteps of farming parents and had learned by helping.

In the vegetable garden my mother did everything with hand tools, except that Father did the first ground-breaking with a small plow behind the tractor. Then Mother came with her rake, smoothed off the surface, broke up the clods of dirt, and removed any sticks or debris that remained. Next, using her hoe, she made rows of fairly deep drills into which she dropped the seeds, then pulled soil over them with the hoe. In earliest spring there would be onion sets and a makeshift frame near the windmill and the livestock water tanks where she broadcast the seeds of lettuce for salads and mustard for greens (which she boiled with fatback, as she did the tender seedlings of lamb's-quarters we picked along the road, Euell Gibbons–fashion). Later, as the weather warmed, she would transplant tomato and sweet-pepper seedlings which she had started indoors a couple of months earlier. And when the ground was thoroughly warm she would put in the seeds for okra and green beans.

The truck patch was a family effort. Father cultivated the ground with tractor and plow, then sowed the seeds with a row-crop planter pulled behind the tractor. If the rains came, the seeds would sprout, along with a tremendous number of weeds. He would go back into the patch with tractor and cultivator to clear out the weeds between the rows, but to get the weeds that grew within the planted rows my mother had to use the hoe. As I grew older I hoed along with her, something I never really liked doing because it was hot, dusty, hard work. I was always glad when the corn got tall; sometimes I would hide in its shade until my mother discovered I was not doing my share of the hoeing.

My second house plant, a pink-flowered *Oxalis crassipes,* now called *rubra,* was given to me when we visited my Great Aunt Eulice the summer I was four. By then I was fascinated by all house plants and anyone who grew them. From the moment my aunt matter-of-factly unpotted her big oxalis, broke it in two, repotted both parts, and gave me the larger, she became my favorite aunt. The two-hour trip home in our pickup truck was unbearably hot, and by the time we turned down our road we were all wilted, especially the oxalis. I shared a big drink of water with the oxalis, and soon its leaves stood up straight. By the next day the plant was once again covered with pink flowers.

Thirty years later the progeny of the same oxalis plant still grow in my parents' greenhouse. One reason this oxalis has survived is that it grows from a fleshy rhizome, or tuber, that stores up moisture. Should you forget to water it for six months, all the leaves will die, but within five days after soaking the soil again you will see sprouts of new green growth. In a month's time there will be pink flowers—provided you continue to add water when the surface soil feels dry to the touch of your fingers. In my city apartment I have a plant of the same kind of oxalis growing six inches below two 40-watt fluorescent bulbs that burn sixteen hours out of every twenty-four. For over a year the plant has been covered with pink flowers, day in and day out.

By my fifth birthday other friends and relatives besides Aunt Eulice knew that I was uncommonly interested in house plants, so my sunny kitchen was filled with wax begonias, a geranium, and some coleus, along with the pink oxalis. No matter how windy and brown it was outdoors, I had my own little world that was always green.

By my ninth birthday, in 1946, books had become an important part of my life, especially books by or about Luther Burbank and the breeding work he had done with flowers and vegetables. I found these in my school library, and by getting myself elected librarian I was able to read and reread the Burbank books at home for most of the school year.

Flowers had already become a passion with me. I helped my parents as much as they asked, but my heart was in the flowers they allowed me to plant. My father had all he could do to look after the farm crops and the cattle; my mother worked ceaselessly taking care of the vegetable garden, truck patch, and chickens, not to mention milking the cows. Obviously neither of them had time for frills, but some of our few neighbors had flowers, and when I went with my parents on their infrequent visits I hinted strongly, or asked outright, for cuttings or divisions. I eventually filled a sizable garden space with flags (German iris), lilacs, and a Harison's Yellow rose—a thorny, May-blooming variety that, as I learned years later, is actually a fine old shrub rose. And I had lots of zinnias, which grew to perfection in our climate because the air was too dry for powdery mildew to attack them.

Then I discovered *Flower Grower* magazine, an event that was to have a major influence on my life. Grandma King, my mother's mother, who lived about fifteen miles away, loved flowers more than anyone else in our family, and in a rare moment of self assertiveness she made a secret pact with me. Whenever I wanted seeds, plants, bulbs, or gardening books or magazines, I was to tell her and she would secretly pay for them out of her weekly household allowance. I was under the impression that Grandfather paid for everything she needed anyway, so I was delighted to accept her offer.

Our secret lasted about two weeks—until parcels of books began to arrive from New York. There must have been at least a dozen, but three stand out in my mind: *Begonias for American Gardens,* by Helen Krauss; *Winter Flowers in the Sun-heated Pit and Greenhouse,* by Kathryn Taylor and Edith Gregg; and *Dianthus,* a monograph by Liberty Hyde Bailey. When my parents discovered my funding source they cautioned me not to spend too much of Grandma's money, but nothing else was said until bank statement time. I hadn't thought about that problem, but Grandma probably had. In any case, she must have stood her ground firmly when Grandfather King questioned her. The next time I was alone with my grandparents, Grandfather gave us both a stern lecture about not spending money foolishly while Grandma smiled reassuringly at me. Then his tone changed and he went on to say that books were great friends, always to be treated with respect. And with that, he proceeded to take a bottle of cold beer out of the icebox, open it, and pour it into a tall glass. I knew Grandfather "drank," though I wasn't supposed to know, but I was amazed when Grandma took the first sip, and flabbergasted when she passed the glass to me and said, "Taste the foam." Since alcohol was an unmentionable at my house, I was sure I was on the road to ruin, but Grandfather took the glass from me and said, "Now we have a little secret from your mother." With that he tipped the glass in a toast to Grandma and me and announced that together they would continue buying the books and other things I needed to grow flowers.

Although I couldn't have realized it then, plants were clearly moving me in the direction of a career. Through addresses I found in *Flower Grower,* I discovered that gardeners all over the country could subscribe to small gardening newsletters or bulletins, and in these exchange their ideas about different plants, join round-robin correspondence groups, and even trade seeds, bulbs, cuttings, and plants. I got into this in a big way and soon had pen pals all over the United States and in some foreign countries.

By the summer of 1946 I had read the Taylor and Gregg book backwards and forwards. I thought these women's adventures with sun-heated pit greenhouses were the most exciting things I had ever heard about. If they and their husbands could dig a pit in the ground and build an A-frame over it with a cold-frame sash covering the side facing south and an insulated roof shielding the side facing north, why couldn't I? After all, they lived near Wellesley, Massachusetts, and according to a map I found in one of my father's farm books, it got cold there much the same as it did where we lived. Father had just joined two old houses together to make a new one for us, and there were plenty of old window sashes to spare.

Since no children lived close enough to be my playmates, I had to entertain myself during summer vacations. One hot morning after both my parents had packed their lunch and gone to the fields, I walked the mile to Grandmother McDonald's house to borrow the sharpshooter spade she used to dig up her vegetable garden in the spring. Getting her to say yes took some fast talking; I was not known for promptly returning tools to their proper places. But she weakened and I was soon skipping back down the road and across the cow pasture to our house. By nightfall I was going to have my own sun-heated pit greenhouse.

My ground-breaking ceremony was more like an attack. The spot I had optimistically staked out for what was to be my eight- by sixteen-foot sun-heated pit greenhouse, the same as in the book, was covered with well-established buffalo-grass sod. By the time I had whacked away one little patch, it occurred to me that maybe eight by six feet was more my size.

The day wore on, as did blisters on my hands, but I kept digging, determined to finish the hole in the ground and build the top before my parents came home. If I had asked before, I was sure they would have said no, or my father would have said, "Yes, but you'll have to wait until I catch up with the farm work so I can help you." Since he, like most farmers of that era, never got caught up, I figured the only way I could have my greenhouse was to surprise my parents with the completed structure. And that is more or less what I did.

Less is more accurate than more here, because the Oklahoma subsoil, which began a few inches below the scene of my battle with the buffalo-grass roots, was as hard as concrete. Instead of digging the entire pit three or four feet deep, as I should have, I decided to dig a trench just wide enough and deep enough for me to work inside it without having to stoop. I could use the bare soil on either side as benches to hold flower-pots.

I don't remember what happened when my parents discovered what I had built that day, which probably means that my father smiled and asked me if I had put away his saw and hammer, and Mother must have said, in her best mock-scolding voice, that I would have to paint the wood if I expected her to look out the kitchen window at the greenhouse while she washed the dishes. The rest of the summer I painted, caulked, shingled, and insulated. By frost time my sun-heated pit was ready to receive all the pots of flower seedlings from the seed-bed I had rigged up in the shade of a lone Chinese elm behind the dugout. There were clarkia and forget-me-not, nemesia and pansy, snapdragon and larkspur—plus rooted cuttings and divisions of geranium, begonia, oxalis, and amaryllis which had come from friends and relatives.

All went beautifully until a week before Christmas, when we had a blizzard. The wind whipped the snow into giant drifts that covered the car and the pickup and swirled to the eaves of the chicken houses. But no snow wrapped its blanket around my little greenhouse, because the wind was blowing the wrong way. Toward nightfall we heard warnings on the radio to prepare for temperatures in the neighborhood of 20 degrees below zero. While Father fed the livestock, Mother and I took care of the chickens, then we found two kerosene lanterns, which we lighted and placed inside my greenhouse. After that we covered the greenhouse with several old blankets and tied them down with rope to keep the wind from blowing them away as it had the snow.

It was a noble effort, but, sad to say, everything inside the greenhouse was frozen solid the next morning. That was the end of my winter flower-growing in a sun-heated pit. One warm day the next spring I tore down the A-frame, put away the window sashes, and filled up the hole. I spared no effort in burying the evidence of the disappointing reality that had followed my summer dreams.

Fortunately, the plants in the greenhouse were not all I had to occupy my green thumbs that winter. The window sills in our new house held all kinds of treasures—and a major challenge. Gardening magazines had been filled that year with news of what one author described as "a harmless but infectious disease," referring to the craze for African violets that was sweeping America. Likening plants to a disease made absolutely no sense to me, and although my mother tried to explain what the author meant, I refused to accept the comparison.

Naturally, I had ordered six different African violets, which were waiting for me in the mailbox one afternoon in September. I opened the carton enough to see what was inside, and then ran all the way to the house. After I had unwrapped, admired, and watered the plants, I read the instructions that were packed with them and decided they should do well on a table next to the sunny kitchen windows. To provide humidity, Mother allowed me to appropriate one of her cookie trays, which I filled with coarse sand and water. The six plants fit perfectly in the tray and, with my usual optimism, I saw the beginnings of a local epidemic.

I waited and watched a week, a month, two months—nothing happened. By Christmas the African violets were beginning to annoy me, a feeling I had never before experienced with plants. If the disease was so infectious, why wasn't I catching it? Mother said to stop fussing, the violets were just getting accustomed to their new home. Then she put her arm around my shoulders as we stood in front of what I thought must be very stubborn plants, and said, "Son, you have to learn to be more patient." My mother often squeezed my shoulders while giving me good advice, but never before in reference to plants. This time it stuck. I began to understand more than African violets.

A few days earlier, when I found my greenhouse frozen, Mother could have said it was all my fault and been right, but she was the kind of parent who knew when it was wrong to be right. Her timing was beautiful. That was the moment when I realized that my greenhouse had needed more patience in the summer and not more heat in the winter to keep it from freezing.

The next day was Christmas, and one of the gifts I found under the tree was a book, *The African Violet,* subtitled *America's Favorite House Plant,* by Helen Van Pelt Wilson, my latest idol among garden writers. I often took the flashlight to bed with me so I could read about Nancy Drew or the Hardy boys' latest escapades, but that night, I read *The African Violet.* The next morning I spied a different-looking new growth at the base of one violet leaf, and by the end of January every plant was covered with blooms. My African violet epidemic has lasted to this day.

2 ❦ Everyday Stress

How important is it to our emotional well-being to have daily contact with nature? To experience the peace and solitude of a garden, or feel the relaxation of a walk through the park? These intangibles cannot be analyzed by a computer, but if, as has been said, the maturity of a community can be measured by the quality of its gardens, our growing concern for plants and nature is a very healthy sign.

If you live in an urban environment, as I do, your alienation from the earth is real, and it really increases the higher up you live in an apartment house. We might even say that the need for living plants increases with the magnitude of the floor number, and this applies to offices as well.

Along with the trend to high-rise living I see a swing to the natural—in foods, furniture, fashion, even in behavior. We want to be more honest with ourselves so that we can deal more realistically with life. Drugs and alcohol may be used as brief escapes from reality, but no one should want to depend on them.

Traditional psychotherapy is sought by some, others seek the answer in transcendental meditation and other forms of consciousness raising.

To whatever discipline the word "therapy" is applied, we tend to think—or hope—that it will work magic in our lives. I maintain that there are no instant cures to life's ups and downs, but rather "supportive holds" that help us put daily difficulties and annoyances into a proper perspective. An involvement with plants can be such a supportive hold.

If you live and work with plants around you, there is always something that needs to be done for them and that will simultaneously help you get through everyday anxieties. As you wait for an important telephone call or recover from a difficult personal or professional confrontation, picking off dead leaves and flowers, watering a plant, or cleaning its leaves with a damp tissue can reduce anxiety far better than chain smoking, a stiff drink, or a tranquilizer.

The more I recognize the symptoms of stress in my life, the more I realize that plants suffer stresses too. Concerning myself with relieving theirs helps me to forget, and thus relax, the tightness in my own body as I nurture my plants.

Putting this into practice in one's own life doesn't require a a whole roomful of plants. It takes only a few to give a range of plant stresses sufficient to relieve your own. Even a single plant may suffer a whole range of stresses in a relatively short time—the need for more or less water, more or less fertilizer, more or less light, a smaller or larger pot, a different growing medium, protection from hot and dry or cold drafts of air, and for protection from insect invasions. The greater your attention to these needs, the greater will be your sense of gratification when your plants thrive.

The more involved you become with your plants, the more

you will identify with them. They have cyclical needs just as we do. When the leaves of a prayer plant or oxalis fold up at night, the plant is resting. After a period of leaf growth and flowering, bulbs like amaryllis and gloxinia go into dormancy for weeks or months. If plants take a rest every night, and require an annual vacation, it seems obvious to me that I need a similar regimen if I am to be healthy and productive.

Although I have always lived with plants, the importance they play in my environment has increased dramatically since 1973, when I moved to an apartment whose windows all faced south. Some afternoon sun is blocked by a building across the street, but the apartment still receives enough light for me to grow Chinese evergreen, Warneckei dracaena, and a well-adjusted polyscias as much as twelve feet back from the windows. In the windows I can grow almost anything, including cacti and other succulents.

I couldn't really afford to move. I simply felt that I must, because of two typically urban environmental traumas. First, as I walked along my familiar city paths, the insidious grime and litter began to depress me. I actually fantasized giving up writing one day a week to clean up and plant the block I lived on. Some writers will do anything to justify not writing, but this fantasy was based on a genuine sense of deprivation.

The second trauma had to do with my own apartment, which had only north-facing windows through which very little light came. Strong, healthy plants looked great in my apartment—for about a week. Then the leaves began to turn yellow, and any new growth was mostly spindly and weak. For more than a year I nursed those poor plants, but despite all my care most of them died simply from lack of light. I kept the good clay and white plastic pots; everything else went down the incinerator. Each time I opened the pantry and saw all those empty pots,

I was reminded of all the incinerated plants. I felt that I was a fraud as a gardening authority. Worse, I felt like a plant murderer.

Indoors or outdoors my environment was equally depressing. It was clear that I had to try as hard as possible to move to a brighter apartment. And ever since I moved I have used plants as major home furnishings. In fact, they represent the largest single investment in the apartment except the Steinway. The inherited carpeting is wall-to-wall green, something we might not have thought of, and everything else is some shade of green on purpose, from pale lime to dark palm frond, with creamy white walls and lots of soft pink and a yellow that's encouraging but not pushy.

The living room in particular had an immediate and powerful effect on me and my family. It was like magic to come from the chaos of the street, ride up in the elevator, and walk into this peaceful indoor garden. I began to realize that walking on the street below didn't matter so much; it is a fact of my life that must be endured. If having an indoor garden at home makes all of us feel better, all the money it cost to move was well spent.

When my present apartment was finally decorated—one might say vegetated—I began to invite guests other than family and friends, and I discovered that *everyone* enjoyed the plants. Decorators pronounced it the wave of the future, magazine editors and book authors brought photographers, models came for fashion photography. But the friends of my teenage children gave my apartment mate, Bill Mulligan, and me a more lasting compliment—they wanted to be with us more. "Wow," "Cool," "Faaar-out," and "Neat" gave way to serious conversations about life. Plants had bridged the generation gap.

Bill and I soon realized that the energy we felt from the plants reached out to every person who walked through our door. And the more I live surrounded by plants, the more certain I am of this: They offer a source of energy anyone can tap.

Until recently I believed that most of the day-to-day tensions and anxieties I felt were of my own creation, and therefore something I could cope with. Now I feel another kind of stress over which I have no control. It is the feeling that disaster from outside can strike at any moment. A bank on my street was bombed early one morning; I had walked in front of it minutes before. A week later, friends and I returned from dinner and went upstairs to sit on the terrace that belongs to one of them; as we walked into the apartment we heard gunshots. At that instant, on the street where we had just walked, one young man was killed and another seriously injured in a fracas with the police. The next evening the theater on my block was robbed; the noise we heard at the dinner table meant that two innocent moviegoers had been killed.

Life is presenting us with increasingly difficult and complex problems. Plants are not necessarily the answer to all personal problems or to the tensions felt from outside, but for sure, involvement with plants can help you cope. Today's craze for plants is no fad. Fads are plastic, plants are real. Although involvement with plants may at first seem merely an escape from life's harsher realities, it is in fact a natural tranquilizer that can enable you to live life more serenely and fully on a day-to-day basis.

Although plants must have been having a therapeutic effect on me all my life, I was not consciously aware of this until 1965, when I was writing a book called *The Flowering Greenhouse Day by Day*. As part of my research I sent a lengthy questionnaire to five hundred owners of home greenhouses. In a brief covering form letter I explained why I needed the answers, but I offered nothing in return for the considerable amount of time it would take to fill out the questionnaire. The response, by return mail, was enormous, and most surprising was the number of doctors who in one way or another said, "I work in my greenhouse to relieve tension, especially late at night when I return from an emergency call."

What the doctors said made sense to me. At the time I was editor of *Park's Floral Magazine,* had finished two books, and was working on my third. In addition, I was director of a large church music program, had gone back to music school, and was preparing for the Metropolitan Opera auditions. At home I was husband, father of three young children, and chief grounds-keeper of a huge lawn and a seemingly endless flower border with enough crabgrass in it to fill every summer weekend. Life was hectic and full of stresses, but I was happy, in part, I am sure, because of the quiet times I spent in my greenhouse.

Looking back, I realize that most of my life I have intuitively turned to plants when I felt tense or anxious. When I have a bad day at work, the dry cleaner loses my favorite shirt, or I forget to transfer funds from savings to checking and my rent check bounces, it is natural for me to spend some extra time with my plants. Writing this book has made me stop and think why it is natural, and why those questionnaire responses made sense. It has made me remember all the stories I've been told over the years about the extraordinary power of plants in the lives of individuals.

The shining, beautiful thing that stands out is this: The nurturing of plants offers challenges that can be met by anyone at any stage of the game, challenges that therefore become the source of satisfying, fulfilling, and stimulating experiences.

If you want it to be, gardening can be a highly competitive game. Once I wrote a story for *House Beautiful* about a woman who grows topiary trees in a greenhouse hardly big enough for the two of us to stand side by side as she told me the fascinating stories behind each of her living sculptures. They were perfectly kept. Growing tips on the myrtle were not nipped by pinching with clumsy fingers but clipped with the steady precision of a surgeon's hands. The clippings that fell among the plants' leaves were removed with long tweezers so as not to bruise or break another leaf or twig.

Was the topiary woman simply compulsively tidy? I think not. The barn to which the greenhouse was attached was a confusion of stacked and strewn clay pots, berry and mushroom baskets holding yet-to-be cleaned bulbs dug from the garden, and a pile of empty but colorful seed packets that no gardener ever wants to throw away.

As we began to move the plants out of the greenhouse for photography, their owner and keeper told me that topiary was a serious thing for her and her friends, the same as bridge or tennis might be for others. This came as no surprise, because a friend of hers had told me beforehand that the topiaries I was to see had won every major award at flower-show time that spring. But I saw much more in the character lines of the woman's face as she touched each topiary and told me its life story. I could tell that this woman wearing faded dungarees and sensible shoes, with no thought of how her hair looked at the moment, kept peace in her soul right where we stood. Life itself might be chaotic, but she would always have order in her greenhouse.

Of course you don't have to feel sad to have plants and flowers make you feel better. I can think of no stronger testimony than that of Dr. C. F. Menninger, of the Menninger Clinic, in Topeka, Kansas, who wrote:

Peonies are very healthy flowers; they have no aches and pains, they make no outcry and there are no anxious and troubled faces to comfort. They just grow and bloom. That is why I fell more and more in love with them. They have helped me to keep my emotional and intellectual equilibrium. Growing peonies has helped me to satisfy an inborn curiosity to watch things grow. There is a gratification of the sense of sight in color and color combinations, of the sense of smell in perfumes and odors, and of that inner esthetic sense of beauty and charm that has, I believe, made a better physician of me. My whole nature was improved, my horizons widened, and my appreciation increased in a way that aided me in my vocation. Hope never dies in a real gardener's heart. Thousands of scientists have chosen horticulture as a hobby and are the better for it too.

On the other hand, some people allow petty prejudices to keep them from fully enjoying the benefits of gardening. One day while I was photographing a patio in New Orleans, the woman of the house got out of what I had been told was her deathbed to tell me I could not bring pink caladiums into her garden because they were a flower of the lower classes. Having made a hasty exit with my vulgar caladiums and the photographer, I asked him what this meant. It was a classic story of mindless class distinction. Poor folks were supposed to grow plants that grew easily and quickly or else had bright colors and flowers with a heavy fragrance. Proper people grew difficult, refined plants of subtle hue and delicate scent. Whether she was near death or not, the woman was already far out of touch with life.

Human beings have always considered flowers and plants necessities in times of both celebration and mourning. As a child I saw little difference in the flowers at church whether the occasion was a wedding or a funeral. In fact I used to feel guilty when my mind turned away from the minister to a total involvement with the flowers, especially during a funeral. Even then I was unconsciously drawing strength from the reality of fresh flowers. Now we are realizing that flowers and plants can help us through the daily ups and downs of life just as they do in times of extreme happiness or sadness.

One common stress known to most of us is the lovers' quarrel, which may last for a night or for an agonizing period of time. A friend of mine has found one way to help move things back toward at least friendly conversation: he picks up a couple of gardenia flowers, some lily of the valley, or freesias at the florist, and at bedtime secretly puts flowers on either side of the bed, placing them just out of sight but where the fragrance permeates the atmosphere. "This is usually all we need to start laughing and patching things up."

Plants help us improve our environment, make a strange one our own, even, if you will, exert some control over a situation in which we feel helpless. Sometimes when I go on tour and face yet another series of empty, impersonal hotel rooms, I first check in, then I go out and buy a bunch of flowers, the heavier the fragrance the better. It takes only a few freesias or roses—or almost any real flower—to help me escape thinking about all the faceless people who have smoked, drunk, eaten and slept in this space that will be my home for tonight. The actor David McCallum tells me he always buys a few plants to keep in his dressing room and hotel room while on location.

Hospitals, like most hotels, have a way of depersonalizing the individuals who occupy the rooms. Having fresh flowers or a living potted plant by the bed is one way to fight off feeling institutionalized. If you're doing the sending, what is best should depend upon the individual and the situation. If the room is already jammed with flowers, postpone your good intentions until your friend gets home. Personally, I would be overjoyed to receive an unusual plant, or a vase of freesias with their elusive, haunting fragrance. One of the nicest things you can do is select a container that the recipient will treasure and use long after the plant has outgrown it or the flowers have faded.

Of course hotel and hospital rooms are not the only new environments to which we have to adjust. One of the reasons I became a college freshman dropout was that I had decided music, not plants, was to be my career and I had no plants in the house where I lived. I left school at the end of the first semester and spent the rest of that spring and summer working six days a week from dawn to dusk in the greenhouses of Albert Buell, the gloxinia specialist. I felt much better. Then I moved to Kansas City to become an editor of *Flower and Garden* magazine and took a dark basement apartment. Subconsciously it must have been a test to see if I could live without plants, for I should have known that nothing would grow there. A fluorescent-light garden would have been a simple solution, but such gardens were less common then, and to a nineteen-year-old, moving seemed the only answer.

Fortunately, just then I met Irene Gentry, a retired librarian who was about to embark on a year's journey around the world on a freighter. We became friendly through our mutual interest in plants, and she decided I could be entrusted with her house and garden. I cultivated the garden with a vengeance, but most of all I loved the big sunny bay window in the dining room, which I kept full of plants and where I also placed my grand piano. I was still pursuing music by being a full-time opera major at the Conservatory of Music, but plants, garden writing, and editing were back in my life.

I spent endless hours in that dining room, practicing while I watched all kinds of fascinating plants thrive in the sunny window. In part, it was, I realize now, a way of feeling closer to my parents during the difficult time of living without them for the first time. I had grown up singing and playing the piano with plants around me, so the more involved I became with music and plants here, the more secure I felt in my new life as a young adult.

It was during my year in Irene's house that I came home one evening and was met halfway through the living room by an overwhelming fragrance. It was as if someone had spilled a bottle of good perfume. That was my first experience with *Cestrum nocturnum,* a night-blooming jasmine. A few weeks later the *Stephanotis floribundum* charmed me with its fragrance, and not long afterward I discovered the sweet-olive, *Osmanthus fragrans,* whose sweet, elusive scent will haunt me all my life.

This experience taught me that plants are always nice to come home to, but especially if you're not accustomed to living alone. And if you'd like not to live alone, plants just might help you find the right person. One young woman I know who sells plants sold a collection of cissus to an attractive young man who said he had never grown anything in his apartment. "I got good vibrations from him, but said, 'If you neglect these and they die, don't come back to me for sympathy or to buy replacements.'" Some weeks later he came back to tell her the cissus looked great and she did too. "So we went out together, but I knew if I went to his apartment and found the plants dead, I would know instantly he was a fraud instead of finding out by having a painful affair." Fortunately for all concerned, the cissus were in vigorous good health.

Plants can also help you get through the work day, something millions of office gardeners know already. For one thing, height and glass walls often permit more sunlight in office buildings than where most of us live. Plants grow better. They also become part of the office routine. If you don't have the time to do the watering, or have to go out of town, there's always someone to take your place.

Unfortunately, office routine sometimes also breeds boredom

and occasionally brings on a severe anxiety attack. Being bored is not one of my problems, but my life is a series of deadlines, a breeding ground for stress and anxiety. Having plants in my office gives me a ready source of relief.

Writing assignments in general give me a touch of anxiety, especially if the words do not come in a flash. That is when I decide my plants need the works—everything except repotting, which I usually save for letting off steam. Sometimes just the thought of giving myself some time to nurture the plants relieves the tension. By the time I fill the watering can I have to hurry back to my typewriter before the words escape me.

Having a collection of plants in your office can also help you make friends and give you something to talk about besides office gossip. I've noticed that people who have a collection of normally healthy and reasonably well-groomed plants in their offices are in general calmer, more efficient, and easier to deal with than those who have no plants at all or whose plants are sadly neglected.

Skeptics may question some of these examples of plant therapy, but one example can't be faulted: I never smoke cigarettes while working with my plants. If I ever stop smoking, which seems especially difficult for writers to do, it will be on a long vacation in the country, when I have the time and the facilities for gardening all day until I fall in bed exhausted every night. Then maybe I will lose a bad habit and gain a beautiful garden.

Stress, anxiety, tension—they are all a part of living and have always been. It's just that today we are living faster and longer, and we are trying to accomplish more in business as well as personal relationships. Although the obvious answer to your problems and mine may be to take a vacation, to work less, or to live in a less urbanized society, none of these options may be ours. Plants are a natural alternative available to all. They can help us get through a tough day, a lonely night, or a long period of anxiety. When you're on top of the world, having plants can make life even sweeter, and when you come down, they'll be a support to you.

Plant therapy requires no prescription. It can be refilled as often as you feel the need. Addiction to gardening, indoors or outdoors, one plant or a thousand, is a desirable state.

3 ❧ Green for the Blues

❧ Most people feel depressed at times, but many of us find it hard to admit. Those who are depressed enough to see a doctor often feel guilty about it: "There must be something wrong with me."

Learning to accept your lows along with your highs is crucial to an overall state of emotional well-being. Perhaps the terrain of life is most interesting as a series of rolling hills and valleys. The flat sameness of a plateau would be boring in time, but existing in extremes from precipitous mountain peaks to dark, cavernous depths is to risk serious emotional traumas.

One of the reasons we have difficulty in dealing with everyday depression is that it usually strikes unexpectedly. In my own experience, I can't work my way out of a downer until I accept the reality of feeling depressed. Although the fall is likely to be rapid, the trip back up to a feeling of well-being is often a step-by-step building process, potentially both productive and rewarding.

Because everyday depression strikes suddenly, it may seem to come out of nowhere, but almost always there is a definite cause, sometimes of your own making but not necessarily. Feelings of inadequacy and failure may be rooted in setting unrealistic goals for yourself, but being fired from a job because your company is moving is something beyond your control. There are large and small reasons for the blues—feelings of not being loved or appreciated, social slights, being passed over for a business promotion, animosities or hostilities directed at us, growing old, winter doldrums and Christmas bills, minor setbacks in recovery from a serious illness—and the times when everything simply seems to go wrong.

Plants can help get you through the initial, crucial period of realizing and accepting depression. Gardeners are by nature optimists. To bury a brown, dead-looking seed or bulb in the ground, all the while dreaming of the beautiful plant it is going to produce, is to cultivate a healthy fantasy life based on the possible, not the impossible.

Professional therapists say that motivation is the first step in treating severe depression and that while patients who have gardened before are usually the first to respond to horticultural therapy, it can work equal wonders for the person who has never been involved with plants. Rhea McCandliss, who pioneered in this work at the Menninger Clinic, tells the story of a young woman who had for several years avoided getting involved in a therapeutic program:

She was given one more chance by her doctor to follow a new plan, which included two hours a day at the greenhouse. Soon reports were that she was again missing some activities, but she was coming regularly to the greenhouse. Why? I will quote her, "Well, you know if I missed a day those seeds I planted might come up and I would not know it, and they might need me to do something for them like give them more light or water or something." When she went home her luggage consisted of as many boxes of plants as it did of clothes.

If plants can help turn life around for the person who has been hospitalized for severe depression, think of how effective they can be in treating common everyday blues.

I once had a serious and painful infection that slowed my work but did not stop me from meeting a deadline—not until I received a carbon copy of a scathing memorandum sent to one of my editors by another, criticizing me unfairly. This flimsy piece of paper depressed me to such an extent that my combined physical and emotional pains sent me home. The few blocks to my apartment seemed like miles. Only the thought of going to bed and forgetting it all kept me trudging along.

Then someming wonderful happened. When I opened my apartment door, I saw a field of wheat glowing as if lighted by an Oklahoma harvest moon. My son Steven and my friend Bill Mulligan had arranged stems of dried wheat in the top of a Plexiglas pedestal, spotlighted from above. The florists' foam that held the wheat in precision-straight rows was concealed by beach sand—with one sea shell placed just so. I felt better instantly.

Next I saw that a box of plants had arrived from Florida. With my coat still on, I began to pry open the carton. Wedged inside were two orchids wrapped against the cold in layers of plastic foam. When finally the first plant could be cradled in my hands, I discovered its clay pot shattered, a broken leaf, and most of the fir bark in which it had been growing spilled on the kitchen floor. As soon as I had misted the battered plant with tepid water, it seemed to look better. A good feeling came over me; I was holding a new plant friend. I put it down gently in a corner of the sink, hung up my coat, and began to unwrap the other bundle. Although they had traveled together in the same carton, the second orchid showed no signs of travel stress. Nestled in the same kind of soft, shredded paper I found a glorious phalaenopsis, its buds bursting to bloom. In the process of finding a clay orchid pot (with special drainage cuts in the sides) for repotting the first plant, and placing both of them in my fluorescent-light garden, I saw that my miniature gloxinias looked pale and wilted for lack of water and the coleus tops needed to be pinched back from the light tubes. I also found the first flower bud on an African violet seedling. At this point my daughter Jeannene came up behind me, and as we stood in front of the lighted shelves of plants with our arms around each other she said, "What are you doing, Dad?" I could have said, "Taking care of the plants," but that was obvious, so I told her the truth: "Coping with office politics."

The marvelous thing about plants is that they always need us. And when we feel unloved and unwanted, finding a new bud on a plant can be far more cheering than going on a clothes-buying spree or on a binge of eating or drinking. Finding the bud gives you a supportive hold on which to build. Its gratification is lasting and has no bad side effects such as unwanted weight, a hangover, or department-store bills weeks later.

Although plants are not supposed to get the blues, one of mine will occasionally go through a period when nothing good seems to be happening. If I had only one plant and it went into a sulk, I might feel anxious or even depressed by its lack of responsiveness. Since I have so many different plants, there are always enough positive growth responses to give my spirits a lift. The thing to avoid is having more plants than you have time or energy to care for properly. Grooming the right number of plants can be highly therapeutic; having too many plants, with dead leaves and flowers mixed among dusty, soot-covered growth, can of itself be depressing.

The same holds true of an outdoor garden. If you want a

sense of order and a feeling of accomplishment from a few hours' work, concentrate your energies in one small area. Otherwise you may be tempted to go helter-skelter, the result being a lot of hard work and no obvious improvement when you stand back to admire your handiwork.

The daily routines of providing proper light, temperature, humidity, fresh air, and water help keep us in better shape to cope with the stresses and anxieties that go along with living, but other aspects of gardening indoors or outdoors seem especially designed for chasing depression.

New seed catalogs arrive in January, just in time to lift you out of the winter doldrums or post-holiday blues. Although some specialists charge a small fee for their catalogs, often deductible from the first order, some of the largest, most colorful and fascinating catalogs are available just for the asking. Names and addresses of mail-order sources for seeds, bulbs, house plants, nursery stock, garden supplies and equipment are listed in Chapter Eleven.

April 15 is tax time for most people, sure blues for a lot of us, but a busy, happy season for all gardeners. Most indoor plants literally burst into new growth in the spring, and outdoors—well, I hardly need tell you that everything is popping. Spring is a good time to plant most things outdoors, and indoors even seeds normally difficult to sprout and cuttings slow to take root grow like weeds.

The end of summer and back-to-school days can be depressing for any number of reasons, two of the most common being a promising romance that fades as rapidly as your sun tan, or having your children leave home to go off to school. Planting bulbs such as tulips, daffodils, hyacinths, and crocus outdoors in autumn, or setting up an indoor-light garden helps you think of spring, or of having flowers indoors in winter, instead of feeling sad because the carefree days of summer have vanished.

Whether I'm up or down at the beginning, a real grooming, bathing, and repotting session on a weekday night or a quiet weekend afternoon almost always makes me feel by the time I finish that I have had a relaxing vacation. Of course I don't always have the time for this kind of activity, especially when I need it most. Too much work, not enough time in the day, and I become tense; nothing seems to go right. The first thing I know, I feel the blues coming on. I've learned to recognize this trap and have found some relatively quick ways to relax with my plants.

One of the best is to take one large plant and groom it to perfection. A palm is ideal because it is too large to move to the tub for a shower. The only way to clean it is to wipe one leaf at a time on both sides with damp paper toweling or a soft cotton cloth. Next I take a pair of sturdy kitchen shears and cut off any fronds that are completely yellowed or dead, right at the point where each joins the main trunk. Then I use a pair of sharp scissors to trim off every dead leaf tip, not blunt-cutting but shaping each as naturally as my artistic ability allows.

As I tackle each phase of this bathing and grooming, my mind is at first occupied with what I am doing, but the repetitive parts quickly lull my mind into a sort of idling state. The end result is that the palm looks as fresh and healthy as those I have seen in the tropics after a refreshing shower, and that I have shifted my head out of high gear to a speed much more conducive to clear thinking and greater productivity.

Equally effective for helping me get out of a bad mood is dividing and repotting a plant that obviously needs it. When you have a collection of several hundred, as I do, there are always plants needing this kind of attention. First I look for a plant with several stems emerging from the soil—a sansevieria or maranta, for example, or an African violet with more than one crown of leaves—and I carry it to the kitchen sink, having first put the stopper in place so I won't clog the drain with debris. I remove the pot and hold the root ball and some soil in my hands, a therapeutic act in itself since I believe we all have an inherent need for contact with the earth. As I begin to work the soil and roots apart with my fingers, I am able to determine how each separate stem or rosette of leaves relates to the others. Then I can cut or break the various divisions apart in a way that leaves the maximum number of roots attached to each.

When all the divisions have been made, I line them up on the counter and clean out the sink, putting the old soil and debris in the garbage can and scrubbing the original pot until it is clean. Next I select enough pots of about the right size to accommodate all the new divisions and plant each at about the same level it grew before in fresh potting soil, first adding a layer of crushed crockery or pebbles in the bottom for drainage.

Whatever my personal concerns may have been in the beginning, by now I am totally lost in concern for the new plants as I firm the soil about each and apply enough water to be certain the contents of every pot are well moistened. If the divided plant has thin-textured leaves, prone to wilting when the roots are disturbed, I will likely enclose each division in a plastic bag, which serves as a miniature greenhouse. When the leaves show no signs of wilting and growth has resumed, I remove the bags, turn them inside out for any condensed moisture to dry, and store them so that they can be used again for the same purpose.

Sometimes the blues make us think that moving to another house or apartment is the answer. If you know it isn't, and want to channel your fantasizing to a more worthwhile cause, try doing a major overhaul of your indoor garden. Repot everything that needs it; trim off every dead edge or tip you can find on leaves; pick or cut off dead leaves and withered flowers. Carry small plants to the kitchen or bathroom sink and rinse the foliage clean in tepid water (slightly warm to the touch, but not hot) : hold your hand over the top of the pot with the stem or stems between your fingers, and turn the plant upside down to allow the water to cleanse the leaf undersides. Set aside to drain, then return to the indoor garden. Large plants, those not too big to lift, can be cleaned in the bathtub or shower.

If you have a yard, terrace, or fire escape—any place where house plants can be readily moved outdoors in warm weather— give the big ones a refreshing shower in a warm, still rain. However, do not put them out when temperatures are below 60 degrees, or when strong winds are blowing.

After you have your plants repotted in clean pots, all the foliage shining and the fresh flowers looking more beautiful because they are not surrounded by dead ones, stand back and look at what you have. Maybe rearranging the plants around a window or in one end of the room can make you feel you have moved to a more desirable environment. If you have many different kinds of plants, a haphazard way of arranging them can in itself aggravate a bad mood. I don't mean to sound like a know-it-all, but I have been filling my environments with plants for a long time. This is one of the pitfalls I get myself into about twice a year. But after a major cleanup session I feel immensely cheered, knowing that my collection of seven or eight different dracaenas is neatly grouped in one corner, all the ferns have their space, and the orchids are all lined up in the brightest sun, except for the phalaenopsis, which grow about two feet back from the window along the edge of a table.

Pedestals of various heights on which to elevate and display your plants can change your collection from an uninteresting one-level, one-dimensional effect to that of a garden which has been groomed to perfection and then displayed with respect to each plant's size, shape, color, and light requirements. Plant pedestals and display platforms can be made of plywood, then painted, papered, or covered with fabric. Or you can use such found objects as clay flue tiles or clean clay flowerpots placed upside down in stacks of varying heights. You can also purchase pedestals made specifically for plant display. These are available in a wide range of materials and range from relatively inexpensive for ready-made ones to a considerable investment for custom design and construction.

Lighting for special effects is another way you can dramatize the inherent beauty of your house plants. Try a floor canister lamp to shine light up through palm fronds or ficus leaves and cast mysterious tropical shadows on the ceilings. Try a ceiling track light flood or spot directed down on a beautiful plant in full bloom, its pot resting on a floor, table, or pedestal, but be careful to keep spots and floods far enough away from delicate petals and leaves so as not to burn or wither them. Flowers that prefer cooler temperatures than the average house or apartment offers in the winter—cyclamen, amaryllis, azalea, pots of hyacinth, tulip, daffodil and crocus—all these wither more quickly if light of any kind, natural or artificial, causes excessive heat to strike the petals.

From the moment you plant some seeds, you will have something good to look forward to. If it's your first time out, try something easy so that success is practically certain. Some of the easiest indoors are coleus, basil (the herb we eat), impatiens and morning-glory. Outdoors, such large seeds as radish, bean, pea, corn, and squash are nearly fail-safe.

Growing plants from seed is one of the happiest aspects of gardening. It is an act of faith as old as history. Even farmers who sow seeds several times a year, often over hundreds of acres of land, treat the planting of seeds with certain reverence. If you want your act of faith to bear fruit, take time to assemble the necessary containers and a suitable growing medium such as vermiculite (an easy seed starter you can purchase in almost every dime store, plant shop, or garden center). The way I like to use vermiculite for starting seeds is to fill a flowerpot or a small plastic or fiberboard seed flat to within one inch of the top with a mixture of two parts packaged all-purpose potting soil to one part vermiculite. I smooth this out with my fingers, press down gently to settle it in place, and add a half to one inch of vermiculite, allowing a quarter to a half inch at the top of the container for planting and watering. Then I moisten the vermiculite with a gentle trickle of water from the kitchen faucet. Now seeds can be sown.

Planting instructions are printed on almost all seed packets, but one good rule of thumb is to cover seeds to the depth of their own thickness. If they are dust-sized, like African violet, gloxinia, begonia, and petunia, simply sprinkle the tiny seeds over the moistened surface, press lightly with your fingertips, and enclose the entire planting, pot or flat and all, in a clear plastic bag. Seeds larger than dust, but not as large as radish seeds, need a scant single layer of vermiculite to cover them; use a gentle trickle of water to moisten the vermiculite added as a seed cover.

Enclosing all newly planted seed containers in a plastic bag is not a bad idea, no matter what the size of the seeds, but the minute you see the green of seedlings, begin to remove the plastic for a while each day, at first for an hour but eventually increasing the time to all day, replacing the cover at night. This will allow you to provide more direct sun for the seedlings in the daytime but give them nurturing warmth and humidity and freedom from drafts at night. The important thing is not to leave a planting sealed in plastic sitting in direct, hot sunlight for more than a few minutes. If you do, your seedlings may be cooked.

Another way of exercising your faith, or of giving yourself

the feeling of taking advantage of a true bargain, is to make cuttings of favorite plants and watch them grow into mature specimens which you can enjoy living with or giving to others. I find that vermiculite makes a superb rooting medium for the cuttings of almost all house plants. Simply fill a small pot—say two and one-half to four inches in diameter—with vermiculite, moisten well, and poke a hole in the center of the vermiculite to accommodate at least an inch of the cutting's stem. Don't bury any leaves in the medium but be sure that at least one node (that point along the stem where a leaf once grew) is below the surface of the rooting medium.

Some of the easiest cuttings to root are coleus, begonia, geranium, African violet, impatiens, and philodendron. Succeed with these and you will be ready to try almost anything.

What you have to prepare for when you begin to propagate your plants is eventual crowding. A packet of gloxinia seed may contain 100+ seeds. If your technique is right and your timing good, you may wind up with 100+ gloxinia plants, each of which will need at least a four- or five-inch pot in which to bloom some five to seven months later. An abundance like this is often what leads people to become fluorescent-light gardeners or to build a greenhouse.

Living or working in rooms that do not receive enough natural light for plants—or at least not for the number or kinds you like most—can of itself cause depression. Adding fluorescent or incandescent lighting as a supplement to or substitute for natural light can be the answer.

It is fairly easy to determine when a plant is receiving too much direct sunlight. The leaves will bleach a paler than normal green and may develop yellow, brown, or black burn spots. But symptoms of insufficient light are not as easily interpreted. Usually a plant will reach weakly, with spindly growth, toward the source of brightest light. If you don't rotate the pot a quarter-turn every two or three days, the plant will grow entirely one-sided and in time may even tip the pot over or simply collapse over the edge, drained and exhausted from the search for more light.

Ficus trees tend to drop their leaves when moved into insufficient light. Other plants—polyscias and dizygotheca, for example—may drop a lot of leaves when moved from a spot fairly close to a sunny exposure to one perhaps ten to fifteen feet farther into the room. If daytime light is bright enough there to read by, polyscias and dizygotheca will probably adapt in time, but not before they have dropped a considerable quantity of leaves. If you know this is natural for the plant you are growing, it will not be upsetting when it happens. But if a weeping fig drops lots of leaves within a two- or three-day period, it almost certainly needs more bright light or sun, and the soil itself may have gotten too dry. One of the problems in watering plants that grow in large tubs is that at watering time only pockets of the soil may absorb moisture, while parts in the pot remain bone dry. The symptoms: some branches of the tree will die suddenly, almost overnight, while others will remain perfectly healthy.

All you need to be an under-light gardener is one fluorescent reflector unit that holds either two 20-watt tubes or two 40-watt tubes placed approximately twelve to twenty-four inches above the table, shelf, or other surface that holds the plants. You can use a combination of ordinary Cool White and Warm White fluorescent tubes, one of each per unit, or you can use one Cool White in combination with a broad-spectrum horticultural tube, such as Gro-Lux Wide Spectrum. The lights need to be burned about fourteen to sixteen hours out of every twenty-four, and it will help relieve your mind if you use an automatic timer. This assures days and nights of uniform length for the plants, and means you won't have to worry about who is going to make the artificial sun shine on your plants on the weekends when you've gone out to find the real sun on the beach. What you should avoid are so-called fluorescent-light gardens which in fact have a puny 15-watt tube, hardly strong enough to be of benefit to any plant.

Ordinary table-lamp incandescent bulbs can benefit plants placed on a table or desk within the lamp's circle of brightest light. If it is the sole source of light, the lamp will need to be burned fourteen to sixteen hours daily. Low-light foliage plants such as Chinese evergreen and spider plant, as well as some plants such as *Oxalis regnellii* and wax begonia, may flower in this kind of light. If it is a supplement to natural light, burn the lamp six to eight hours daily, at whatever time is convenient.

Supplementary light for indoor trees, shrubs, and hanging baskets can be provided with incandescent floodlights, generally available in sizes from 75 to 150 watts; use them in porcelain sockets. General Electric's Cool Beam, Sylvania's Cool Lux, and Duro-lite's Plant Lite are excellent. As a supplement to weak natural light, burn them six to eight hours out of every twenty-four; as the sole source of light, fourteen to sixteen hours will be required. Position the floodlight above or to the side of the foliage, two to three feet away, so as not to burn the leaves.

Although the plants you grow, either indoors or outdoors, can be a constant antidote to the blues, sometimes just buying a few fresh-cut flowers can work wonders when you feel out of sorts with yourself or the world in general. There's always room for flowers in any home, and it may be even more rewarding to send a bouquet of flowers or a beautiful plant to a friend you haven't seen recently. Receiving flowers or plants for no particular reason is a spirit lifter for the receiver, not to mention what it does for the sender. Besides, receipt of the gift usually means you will receive a telephone call or a note, and the friendly message may be just what the doctor ordered to pull you out of a funk.

4 ❧ The Angry Gardener

The high-tension lives that most of us lead today make occasional anger and hostility almost inevitable. Failure to get these intense feelings out of our systems can lead to serious emotional difficulties. All too often we vent them on our families or close friends, a bad habit that can also lead to a lot of anguish for all concerned. If you are a gardener, look around you. There's bound to be some hard physical labor or a tedious, repetitive chore such as edging the lawn that will allow you to let off steam and be productive at the same time. This can be immensely satisfying.

I realize now that anger has driven me to the garden for relief more times than I would care to recall. Those were the days when I could go out in the back yard and hoe big weeds; I could jog as I pushed the lawn mower faster and faster; and I could saw and hammer some lumber to make a plant display stand.

Perhaps I'm mellowing with age and don't get as angry any more. Now I find that hammering broken or unusable clay pots into shards helps me dissipate my hostilities. This is a release that is beneficial because I use the shards in lieu of pebbles at the bottom of container plantings to provide air for roots and assure drainage of excess water.

Another way the indoor gardener can sweat off anger is to soak, scrub, and rinse empty flowerpots. Clay in particular develops a build-up of white mineral salts along the rim and outside walls that is not only unsightly but harmful to plants, especially kinds like African violets, whose leaves or leaf stems may rest on the rim. For this job I use soap pads, a stiff scrub brush, and sometimes an old kitchen knife for scraping away the most stubborn encrustations. After all the pots are clean and dry, I store them in neat stacks according to size. This gives an immediate sense of accomplishment which I feel again every time I have need for a fresh pot.

Pruning in the outdoor garden has often been suggested for working out anger, but I have a notion that this idea is associated with the kind of pruning that is grossly insensitive to a plant's natural habits. A bald-headed, harshly clipped forsythia, dotted with a few lonely yellow flowers, is enough to make every gardener who sees it angry himself. I would definitely not prune if I felt really angry, but after moving into the cooling-off stage I think pruning would be just the ticket.

Heavier plant-related work, such as building something for the indoor or outdoor garden, is good for releasing feelings of aggression and hostility. I have met several gardeners who vented their anger by building a greenhouse, and the second of my own childhood greenhouses was a product of positively directed feelings of hostility.

The summer before I entered the sixth grade I felt as angry as any ten-year-old could. A change in the school laws of Oklahoma and Texas meant that next year I would no longer be allowed to attend the "big" school in town. Of course it wasn't all that big, but when you're transferred to a country class numbering eleven pupils, anything would seem bigger and better. My disappointment made me mean; I decided to start the wearing-down process the day school was out, using the whole summer, if necessary, to convince my parents that they should pay for my tuition in town. But they stood so firm that by June I decided I had better find another outlet. I wouldn't try another pit greenhouse; this time I would try another, more elaborate kind that was also described in *Winter Flowers in the Sun-heated Pit and Greenhouse*. I could tell from what the authors said that we had the perfect spot for a lean-to greenhouse on the south-facing wall of the dugout where we used to sleep, which was about fifteen skips from the front door of our new house. This time I would try to be more patient in the building, but I was certainly impatient to *start*. And I didn't know exactly how, or what with.

I had all this on my mind one day when I went with my father to the lumber yard. While he took care of business I snooped among the kegs of nails and shiny pails of paint. And I stopped to look at the rack filled with rolls of the celluloid-covered wire mesh I had helped my mother use to winterize the windows in our chicken houses. Then it happened. Right next to the rack I saw a pamphlet with a picture of a lean-to greenhouse on the front. In an instant the pamphlet was in my hands and I was reading. Yes, of course, these inexpensive window-covering materials could be used to keep more than chickens warm in the winter. There were diagrams and step-by-step instructions showing and telling exactly how to build the lean-to greenhouse I had been thinking about. By then my father had said for the third time, "Son, let's go." Seeing that there was a stack of pamphlets left, I stuffed mine in my pocket and raced to catch up with him.

I read the pamphlet to my father on the way home, and since

we were in the old pickup truck loaded down with lumber, the sixteen miles, mostly on bumpy dirt roads, gave me plenty of time to convince my captive audience that we should build this greenhouse. His teasing attitude made me 99 percent sure from the start that the answer would be yes, so I played along, presenting my case with appropriate fervor. As we turned in the driveway, I knew that one day soon the bare wall I was looking at would be covered with a lean-to greenhouse.

I put my plans on paper, carefully adapting from those in the pamphlet. Six by nine feet seemed to be the right size for the wall space we had. My father showed me how to dig the trench for the foundation, how to build the forms, and then how to mix and pour the concrete. A few days later we removed the forms and bolted two-by-six wood sill plates on top of the foundation. Then Father got me started with the two-by-fours that shaped the walls and roof, and I finished the rest, except for the door, which required his more craftsmanlike carpentry. When the framework was all nailed in place, I gave it two coats of white paint and then tacked the celluloid-covered wire mesh in place. Before frost my mother and I went to town and found a bathroom-size gas heater with a thermostat and my father took time off from field work to install it. I was ready for a great cold-weather adventure. And I was beginning to think I might like the new school.

Some satisfying tactile release is often all many of us need to overcome minor anger and frustration. Mixing and squeezing potting mediums of varying textures is a viable source of this release and one I've tapped many times since the farm days when my hands were often digging into and mixing large quantities of soil.

One of the sharpest-textured potting ingredients is perlite, and this is not so surprising when you consider that it is often used as a substitute for "clean sharp sand" when the sand is not available for the recipe being mixed. One way it is sometimes used is to mix one part perlite to two or three parts packaged, all-purpose potting soil that seems too fine-textured and dense to drain well. I have intentionally said, "two or three parts" in my simple recipe, because when you're mixing potting ingredients, the measurements can be approximate. Since you know the perlite serves as a substitute for sand, and both are used to improve drainage, it follows that less perlite should go into a mix for foliage plants than in a mix for desert cacti. I've never used measuring cups. I'm more likely to pick up a clay flowerpot to use as my scooper and measurer. Through experience I've learned that a five-inch standard flowerpot holds approximately one quart of soil-mix ingredients.

Charcoal chips also have a certain hard-edge feel to the hands. They are most often used as a sprinkling over the bottom layer of drainage material placed in any container that does not have a hole in the bottom. The purpose of the charcoal is to help keep excessively moist or poorly aerated soil fresher.

Vermiculite has a nice spongy, flaky feel to it. It has been one of my favorite growing mediums most of my life. The easiest way to use vermiculite is to fill a flowerpot or seed flat with it, moisten well, then plant cuttings or seeds and enclose the planting in plastic. Because vermiculite, like perlite, is a sterile planting medium, the chance of seeds or cuttings succumbing to a fungus disease is drastically reduced. Vermiculite is sometimes used in improving all-purpose packaged potting soils. Since vermiculite tends to hold moisture while permitting aeration of the soil, it is especially useful in mixing soil for plants that seem to enjoy a spongy growing medium. Years ago well-rotted leaf mold would have been used, but there's not much of that in cities these days.

To mix a batch of soil you might use for potting a begonia or almost any other flowering plant, use this recipe: one part *each* of vermiculite, packaged all-purpose potting soil, sphagnum peat moss, and perlite. Gesneriads may do better if you use two parts vermiculite to one each of the other three ingredients.

There is more than one kind of peat moss, but my preference for potting mixtures is one labeled "sphagnum peat moss." It is medium brown, fibrous, and spongy; water saturation changes the color to dark brown. In the paragraph above I suggested one use for peat moss. If you have inherited a plant that needs an acid soil, and you want to repot it in fresh soil, here is a recipe: three parts sphagnum peat moss to one *each* of perlite, vermiculite, and all-purpose packaged potting soil. This should be good for citrus, gardenia, azalea, and African violet.

I always enjoy trying new combinations, and sometimes I discover that a mix altered only slightly will produce better results than before—maybe not spectacularly different, but enough for me to try yet another variation. I get a little lift when something works well and a small letdown when an experiment fails. But I have lots of plants. Only if grossly neglected would *all* of them curl up and die. I have a lot of confidence in my plants and they in me.

And it may make you happy to know that you can grow plants without mixing potting soils at all. There are prepackaged mixtures formulated for foliage plants, terrariums, African violets, and desert plants (cacti and succulents). Packaged African violet mixes are likely to be on the acid side, and therefore a good choice also for potting up citrus, gardenia, and azalea.

To tell the truth, the most important problem you are likely ever to encounter with potting soil is how to tell when it's wet, moist, or dry. Most house plants do well in a range from briefly saturated (pour off excess water left in saucer within an hour or two) to not quite on the dry side. If you develop the tactu-

ally satisfying habit of pinching the top half inch or so of potting soil around each of your plants, you will soon gain a sense
of what soils of varying moisture content feel like.

What has caused more trouble than any other advice handed
out about plants, and I think appropriately included in a chapter on the angry gardener, is the instruction that reads: "Let
this plant dry out completely between waterings." This kind of
advice is scandalous. Even desert cacti and succulents, if left in
pots indoors during the winter until the soil was *completely*
dry, might suffer enough internal stress to become unable to
accept water again. When you do water such a plant, you will
only hasten its total disintegration. What causes about 75 percent of the dead leaf tips and edges among indoor plants is allowing the soil to dry out too much between waterings; chalk
up the rest to overwatering, overfeeding, lack of humidity, or
too much or too little sunlight. Neglect in the form of any of
these is hostility directed *at* plants rather than being released
through concern *for* them.

There are three growing mediums I have not yet mentioned,
and all are coming into increasingly common use by amateur
growers. Two are osmunda fiber and fir-bark chips, both used
for growing orchids and bromeliads. A staghorn fern is often
mounted on a wooden plaque with osmunda fiber placed between the two. Small bromeliads, *Tillandsia ionantha*, for example, may be cultivated with their roots fastened to a chunk
of osmunda fiber or tree-fern bark. Plants growing in or attached to these mediums, particularly indoors, require special
watering techniques. Soak wall-mounted plaques and containers
of these mediums once every three days, for approximately ten
minutes. Remove and allow to drain, then you can return the
plant to where it was before. To do this I fill my kitchen sink
with tepid water and soak as many plants together as it can
hold.

The other growing medium, called soilless, is lightweight, moisture retentive, perfectly aerated, well drained, and sterile. The trade names used for soilless mixes include Jiffy-Mix (but not the muffin mix of the same name), Redi-Earth, Supersoil, and Pro-Mix, among others. All of these may be used for container plants indoors or outdoors. The main difference in using them is that you will need to feed a little with every watering, mixing the fertilizer at one-fourth to one-fifth the strength you would use for plants growing in ordinary potting soil. In other words, if the label specifies one teaspoon of fertilizer per quart of water, reduce this to one-fourth teaspoon or slightly less per quart of water for a feed-with-every-watering program.

The soilless mixes are based mostly on formulas perfected at Cornell University and the University of California to provide a means of growing container plants without depending on special soils that may become scarce in the future. Recipes vary, but most include sphagnum peat moss, perlite, and vermiculite in a well-balanced mixture. Some are based on shredded fir bark and may include some perlite and charcoal chips.

One soilless mix, called Terralite Tomato Soil, is formulated specifically for tomatoes and may be used to cultivate them in containers, or you can dig out a gallon or two of soil where you want to grow a tomato in the garden and fill up each hole with the Tomato Soil.

Aside from the other good qualities of soilless mixes, their light weight can be a big help to the person who cannot lift heavy containers of standard potting soils. They may also be the answer for a roof-top garden where too much weight could threaten the structure of the building. And no matter how strong you are, carrying big bags of a soilless mix into an apartment building for use indoors or on a terrace is a lot easier than toting the real thing.

So-called cutleaf philodendrons, pothos, numerous true philo-

dendrons, and nephthytis or trileaf wonder are often seen growing as climbers on a piece of rough bark or tree fern placed in
the pot. The trouble with these is that desirable growth tends
to play out as soon as the stems reach the top of the pole and
have nowhere else to fasten their roots. Self-heading philodendrons such as *P. selloum* are a much better choice among large-
size plants, and among the smaller ones pothos, heartleaf and
silverleaf philodendrons, and nephthytis don't seem to resent
being trained into bushy or trailing plants.

Professional horticultural therapists actively use certain aspects of gardening to help patients work off anger and hostility.
Of her work at the Menninger Clinic, Rhea McCandliss writes,
"Sometimes patients come and say, 'Have you any broken pot-
tery I can pound to pieces today, or a weed patch I can chop
out, or something to keep me from exploding?' Then I know
they are learning that there are ways to relieve tension that are
constructively destructive."

Ms. McCandliss' colleague at Menninger's, Andrew Barber,
adds:

In January we start cuttings of our cascade mums and at this
point it is really an educational tool, but laying the groundwork
for the ultimate blooms. All summer we pinch, tie and train. It
is frustrating. One patient when asked what job she liked best
in the greenhouse replied, "pinching the cascade." She often
came to the activity spitting mad. She would volunteer to cut
things back when needed and believe me she had a heavy hand
with the pruning shears. She has been able to control her anger
by many therapeutic experiences and now is a day patient with a
job. She has bloomed like the cascades.

Ms. McCandliss also tells the heartening story of "Patient
B," a young man with a number of problems, some of which
kept him quite isolated from everyone around him:

When he first came to the greenhouse I asked him to keep a record from the daily temperature readings, as the extremes are quite meaningful to us in relation to plant growth and hardiness. The first thing in the morning I would hear the door open and see a streak flash by, as he rushed out to the back to read the thermometer. His extreme compulsiveness meant continuous records for that winter at least. Another job which his compulsivity and desire for isolation made tolerable to him was the daily watering in the greenhouse. I found that spring that no little seedlings would die for lack of water, nor were they flooded with a water stream of fire-hose intensity, since Mr. B. carefully changed to a fog-nozzle each time he watered them. With increasing interest in plant life he built an illuminated plant box in Manual Arts. This he kept in his room. A few months later he proudly, and shyly, presented me with a blooming African-violet plant he had grown from seed, a plant usually considered difficult to flower from seed, in a much longer time. Now he has started back to college to get his degree in "some phase of horticulture, probably to do research."

What this young man learned is something from which a lot of us can benefit. There are times when I too feel compulsive about keeping busy. Picking off dead leaves or transplanting a flat of seedlings to individual pots seems to calm me, as does a lot of vegetable chopping or making an apple pie. And all such activities keep me from smoking, keep me from yelling at my nearest and dearest or getting ulcers trying not to yell. They also, and often sooner rather than later, soothe my sometimes savage breast.

5 ❧ Plants and Crises

All the major crises of life—loss of a loved one through death, estrangement from a spouse or a lover, loss of a job, moving, changing jobs, retirement—have their own emotionally debilitating potential. The shock of any one of these, if not cushioned, can cause an emotional breakdown in the individual experiencing it. And psychologists tell us that the occurrence of any two or three in rapid succession, with little time for recovery in between, is sure-fire trouble unless there is some sort of consolation or diversion.

Gardening, indoors or outdoors, is a proven source of strength in times of great emotional need. Whether an involvement with plants predates a life crisis or develops afterward makes little difference.

The craze for African violets that followed World War II may be an example of widespread use of plants as therapy. Perhaps it is not too far-fetched to say that many people who had lost someone in the war needed something to nurture. The prodigious African violet was perfect. It can be multiplied easily by putting down, as they say, one healthy leaf with a little bit of the stem pressed into moist soil or putting a leaf with a slightly longer stem in a glass of water. Baby plants form at the base of the stem and grow to blooming size in a few months. Then more leaves can become parents. If one plant is allowed to multiply, it can be divided. Pollen from one flower can be dabbed onto the stigma of another; if the mating is successful, a seed pod will form, and eight to ten months later the flowers of the progeny can be eagerly anticipated.

Any plant, but especially those that, like African violets, are cultivated indoors, can help you survive painful personal loss. Indoor plants depend on you for their very existence. People need plants, but just as surely plants need people, and being needed can make the difference between wanting to live and not caring.

The sending of flowers and plants to the home of the bereaved person or to the funeral parlor suggests a long-time awareness of the therapeutic value of fresh flowers and living plants. Although some people criticize the use of cut flowers because they are here today and dead tomorrow, just as surely as the body they memorialize, philosophically they emphasize that death is a part of life in the world of plants as it is in the world of people.

Living plants sent to a grieving person can be the source of emotional support for weeks, months, or years. Since what you send is likely to be strongly associated with thoughts of the person who has died, the usual response is to want to keep the plant alive and healthy as long as possible. If the person to whom you are sending the plant does not know its care, be sure to include clearly written instructions, your own or copied from a book.

In judging the Burlington House Awards for American gar-

dens, I once came across a widower in the South who had multiplied the plants received for his wife's funeral into a memorial
garden open to the public. His loneliness has been at least
partly filled with the care and development of the garden, and
in sharing its ever changing, ever growing rewards with all
who come to visit.

In the notes that accompanied the widower's entry he explained:

> Those plants gave me something to do during the most difficult
> period following my wife's death. In the times when I was
> alone, especially at night when I couldn't sleep, I would fuss
> over each one, being sure the soil in the pot felt moist enough
> when I rubbed some of it between my fingers, and keeping every
> wilted flower and yellowed leaf picked off. In time I found my-
> self thinking less about my loss, and more about what I might
> do with the azaleas. I began to read books and articles, and
> learned how they could be propagated from cuttings. Soon my
> son and I were building a propagating frame outdoors and
> planting cuttings. They required daily attentions. It was a major
> step forward for me when I discovered the first roots.

The most poignant story I know about giving a living plant
to acknowledge death is that of a copperleaf beech called
Johnny's tree. Seventeen-year-old Johnny had committed sui-
cide. A grieved neighbor gave the parents the young tree, and
with other close friends helped the family site and plant it in a
private ceremony after the public burial: "Each of us helped dig
the hole that would cradle and sustain the roots. The thought
that we were planting a young tree which would grow sronger
and taller until its branches created a great canopy, under which
children might play for a hundred years, was tremendously
therapeutic."

A young widow once called me at my office, apologizing for

the disturbance but saying she had to tell me of her experience with plants. Her husband had died suddenly. She was left completely alone and feared she might not be able to cope. Something made her pick up a copy of my *World Book of House Plants* and she began to read the chapter on propagation. One sentence caught and held her eye: "Seeds are miraculous."

"I knew I needed a miracle," she told me, "so I decided to try seeds. By the time I assembled the necessary supplies and selected the seeds, which happened to be impatiens, I felt a glimmer of hope. The night I came home to my empty apartment and discovered the little brown seeds had turned into fresh, green plant babies, I knew that the worst was over." She apologized again for taking my time and told me good-bye before I could tell her how she had made me feel. I remember choosing those three words carefully when I wrote the book; to me they were the most important ones in it. The widow's call meant more to me as an author than she could have imagined; I can only hope that she reads this thank-you.

Indirectly, plants helped me through the emotional crisis of losing my mother. I was in the middle of editing the sixteen-volume *Good Housekeeping Illustrated Encyclopedia of Gardening,* a task that required five careful readings of over a million words before the final proofs were okayed, and thumbing through some 25,000 photographs and pieces of art work. My mind concentrated at all times at many levels as I read typed page after typed page and galley proof after galley proof. Was the Latin spelled and phonetically pronounced correctly? Was the typography properly styled? Did each entry tell exactly how to grow the plant and how to perpetuate it? Was it illustrated by a correctly labeled photograph or illustration? And was the caption in agreement with the text?

Meanwhile my mother's battle with cancer wove its fearsomeness through my mind. I was sustained by reading about

plants of all kinds and daydreaming on occasion of how some-
day I would have time to grow some of them. I spent my
mother's last three weeks sitting in her hospital room, helping
her when I could and reading galleys the rest of the time. That
is exactly what I was doing one afternoon when I sensed a
change in the room. My mother was gone.

The day after the funeral my father and sister and I had to
take care of legal matters, and the next day I said I had to go
back to New York. Only my secretary knew that the reason I
took a flight out of Amarillo to New York via Dallas was that
I was actually flying to New Orleans in order to be alone for
two days. I slept and ate when I felt like it, but mostly I remember walking along the narrow streets of the Vieux Carré,
soaking up the springtime sun and the balmy nighttime. Each
time my nose caught the haunting fragrance of the sweet-olive
trees and bushes my steps took me back to find the source.

Some years later I saw a television special in which Dick
Cavett interviewed Tennessee Williams as they sat on the patio
of the same guest house where I had stayed and rode in a buggy
along the same streets. Cavett asked Williams what made the
air intoxicating in New Orleans, and although neither of them
said they knew, I do. It is the sweet-olive.

Two years later I was in San Francisco on business and received an urgent message from New York to call Bertie Crane,
one of my closest friends, who had moved to southern California about a year earlier. I knew before I heard the words that
her husband had died. Since she and Bill had come to be my
adopted parents, and I had been planning to surprise them with
a visit the next day, the shock was severe. The first thing I did
was change my plane reservations and cancel the day's appoint-
ments, but my mind was racing, trying to find a hold. Then it
came to me. When they moved to California I had inherited

Bill's plants. To this day I never see or touch one of them without feeling more comfortable about life—and death.

When my marriage fell apart I took care of first things first, functioning fairly well in a state of shock. We told the children together, I found an apartment for myself and took the children to see it. A friend who had decided there was no future in being a landlord, and was about to sell his three furnished apartment houses, said he was sure we could find enough old furniture to tide me over. I did some fast painting and papering. I went to Bloomingdale's and bought the newest designer sheets and towels. I arranged to cash checks at the D'Agostino's in my new neighborhood as I stocked up on food and staples. I found some dishes and stainless steel flatware left over from photography at *House Beautiful.* I also worked day and night on the *Good Housekeeping Illustrated Encyclopedia of Gardening.* I was cool. I had begun to put myself back together again and by Friday evening I could pick up the children and bring them to their "other" home for the weekend.

By the time we were in the apartment together fifteen minutes I knew I had forgotten two necessities. There was no can opener and Steven said, "Dad, this place looks sort of bare without any of your plants or flowers."

I hadn't bought plants because I don't like buying plants in a hurry. There simply hadn't been enough time. But if one of my children missed them too, then at least we could have flowers. Thanks to Steven's and Jeannene's remembering the neighborhood all-night florist and Mark's resourceful hammer-and-screwdriver can opener, we had food on the table that night along with glorious yellow and orange-red tulips. Inspired by the tulips, we got the idea of doing a huge abstract painting of them directly on the wall of the new living room. I happened to have masking tape and leftover cans of orange-red and yellow paint. Steven helped with the design and Jeannene with the tape, and Mark photographed us as we worked. The presence of flowers directly and indirectly got us happily through our first night in new surroundings.

Later, after the children had gone to bed, I sat down in the living room, having first poured myself a stiff drink. I lit a cigarette and looked around. Steven was right, the place needed plants. I realized for the first time that now I would have the freedom to grow as many plants as I pleased and to arrange them in a more contemporary fashion than the furnishings of my previous apartment had permitted.

The following Monday an advertising agency called to say they were preparing a campaign for the plant encyclopedia. They planned to photograph me in a jungle of plants; would I go out and select several hundred dollars' worth and have them delivered to the photographer's studio? Well, just the thought made me feel happier than I had for weeks. And when I finished posing as an English gardener with a full beard (mine), tweed jacket, and pipe (theirs), the photographer said, "I'd like to keep one of these plants. Where shall we send the rest?"

I'm sure Steven will agree, that our apartment has never again looked bare.

The postscript to this story is even more surprising. For some reason my wife had decided to keep my plants when we separated. Not many months later she told me she was taking a course in house plants at the Y. These days, when I pick up or drop off one of the children, she occasionally asks me to come up and give her some green-thumb advice. Since my plants became hers they have grown tremendously. The kentia palm we paid $38 for in 1967 would cost a small fortune today, if one of that size could be found. Edith must have always had a green thumb, which she now uses to benefit not only her plants but her own sense of self.

Not long ago I went house hunting with a real estate agent in northwestern Connecticut. We began early one Sunday morning, intending to see as many houses as possible so that I could establish what was available and where, and at approximately what price. We worked hard at looking until midafternoon and then decided it was time to break for lunch. As we waited in the restaurant the agent and I began to talk about ourselves instead of houses.

I discovered a successful businesswoman in her mid-forties whose marriage had gone on the rocks a couple of years earlier. She had turned to house plants for something living to greet her when she came home, something to make her feel needed, regardless of the general state of affairs in her life. Conversations with ex-spouses can be difficult, especially in the area of "What have you been doing?" since this question usually means "Who are you seeing?" On the other hand, some contact is necessary when there are children. The realtor had discovered she could talk about her plants to her former husband and keep the conversation relaxed. It wasn't long before he too began to grow plants, and now they are able to deal with each other civilly as fellow gardeners. Because of this she somehow felt better about the whole experience of marriage, children, marriage troubles, and divorce.

Another newly divorced friend, an editor, called to say that in his new life he wanted to live in a completely different environment. Did I know a good designer (not too expensive, of course) who would approach this new living space from a "with-it" viewpoint? Maybe one who would rely on a modular concept with lots of movable platforms and cushions to form seating and sleeping accommodations, and platforms and pedestals for plant display with supplementary artificial lighting as necessary to sustain their growth. Fortunately, he got what he wanted from the designer I recommended and the editor now credits plants for getting him safely through divorce and into a new life.

Plants may also help a relationship that seems in danger of falling apart. Through my work in the American Gloxinia Society I met two couples, one on the East Coast, the other in the Midwest, who told me quite frankly that gloxinias had been marriage savers for them. The stories were remarkably similar, even though the individuals were completely different in background and personality.

Neither couple had children, and both were approaching middle age. It was panic time all around. Then one party of each couple had seen a beautiful gloxinia in a florist's shop and purchased it. The nurturing of the plant had become a mutual and sharing experience. They began to delve into books and find out more about gloxinias, and, in both instances, an address for the American Gloxinia Society had been found. Soon they were members, more gloxinias were ordered, both as dormant bulbs and hybrid seeds, and a new life was beginning to unfold.

One of the couples lived in a city row house that received little or no direct sun except in one window. The basement eventually became a greenhouse, lighted entirely by rows of fluorescents suspended over double-decker plant benches. The other couple lived in the suburbs in a house very much like the others on the block, surrounded by a lot of lawn that neither of them especially enjoyed maintaining. It also reminded them painfully that their environment was a carbon copy of all those around them, except that the others had children and the promise of grandchildren in the future. Mutual interest in the gloxinia led to the construction of a greenhouse, which completely changed their landscape, and inside the greenhouse gloxinia seedlings, rooting leaf cuttings, and plants in all stages of growth gave them the sense of life affirmation that they had missed.

The purchase of two seemingly insignificant flowering plants changed four lives directly, and indirectly benefited thousands of others. Instead of feeling like local nobodies who did not have the bond of raising children, they became important in the plant world—eventually both husbands served as elected officers in the American Gloxinia Society—and, more important, they had living plants dependent upon them. This new sense of self and responsibility changed the way they felt about their neighbors and the people they worked with. Four lives and two marriages had survived the test of time, thanks to a "growing interest."

Over the years I've known many mothers and fathers who filled their lives with plants after the children grew up and moved away, but women of that age today face another dilemma, summed up in a few words by my Westchester friend Joan Lang, who says,

> I'm one of those women who can't be a housewife any longer and I can't be an outright women's liberationist either. For me, my fluorescent-light garden in the basement represents a whole new outlet, after a lot of years of having to be at a certain place at a certain time or having to take the kids here and there. My basement garden is where I put my two worlds together. It's my domain and responsibility, a place to be sloppy in a regimented world. Gardening there gives me a peaceful, restful feeling. I like the fact that it can be ignored for a day and not fall apart. And I love the quietness in my basement garden which allows me to escape our noise-stressed society.

In today's mobile world plants are one way to help you adjust to another city or a new house or apartment. The kentia palm I described earlier moved with my wife and me three times in a period of two years. There was one house I particularly disliked, and although I don't make a practice of talking with my plants, when the palm suddenly looked like it might die, I got the message. We moved not long afterward and the kentia has lived happily ever since.

I also learned from these frequent moves that the most therapeutic thing we could do the first night, besides set up the beds for everyone, was to hook up the stereo and play some soothing music; in tumultuous times, which I consider moving to be, I like Bach, whose music, like that of other baroque and classical composers, is alleged to be good for plants too. Then I would set up the living room furniture and position the plants where they looked the most attractive. This gave me and the rest of the family one room with some sense of order and a reasonably tranquil atmosphere.

In the times when I have moved cross-country and could not take my plants along, one of the first things I do in the new location is to assess conditions of light and sun in the new environment, and then begin to assemble a collection of plants, usually starting with some of my favorites from the previous residence and adding some new ones I have been wanting to try anyway. This approach has given me the security of having some familiar plants in my new home along with the pleasure of making friends with some new ones.

Although I have never done it, several people have told me they made cuttings of their favorite plants to carry with them to another city, as the pioneers used to do on the way West. One modern method is to wrap the base of each cutting in a piece of water-soaked tissue, then wrap a piece of aluminum foil around this and put it in a plastic bag. Add as many cuttings as the bag will hold comfortably, blow up the bag, and seal it at the top with a rubber band or twist-tie. While in transit, keep the bagged cuttings out of direct sunlight and in temperatures comfortable for you. As soon as you arrive at your destination put the stems of the cuttings in glasses of water. They may be left to root there, or you can plant them in containers of moistened vermiculite.

Friends of mine who are more oriented to gardening out of doors than I moved fourteen times within a few years. "We discovered it made us feel less transient if as a family we planted an evergreen or other shrub on each property as soon as possible after we moved in. The plant would put down deep, permanent roots even though ours were likely to be shallow. We knew we could come back years later—which some of us have done—and see how our landmark had grown."

Loss of work, whether by retirement or otherwise, is highly circumstantial and therefore difficult to discuss generally. The loss of income—and sometimes loss of self-esteem—that results from unemployment and often from retirement cannot be replaced by other satisfactions. What is useful in the context of plants is to know that people who have a hobby or an avocation usually find it easier to cope with loss of work or retirement than those who have no specialized interest. A number of people have told me that having a garden outdoors or a collection of indoor plants kept them occupied and helped them maintain a sense of self-esteem during a period of unemployment.

When it comes to retirement, I think first of my friend Zelma Clarke, who once told me she never had to face waking up that first Monday morning after retirement wondering what to do with the day, or for that matter the rest of her life. Gardening had been her avocation; now she couldn't wait to turn it into a full-time career.

When Zelma retired as executive secretary to the president of a big corporation, her basement was already filled to overflowing with plants growing in tiered shelves of fluorescent lights. Building a greenhouse against her garage was the first project. What has always impressed me most about Zelma, aside from the obvious pleasure she derives from growing plants well, is the sensible plan she follows to have something always coming into bloom in the greenhouse. She uses an old refrigerator to provide the period of darkness and cool temperatures required for rooting spring bulbs to be forced into winter bloom in the greenhouse. Her workbench is as efficiently arranged as the business affairs of her boss must have been. A clip board holds notes of when to plant what; there is a telephone, an intercom to the house, and a radio. Her tools are neatly arranged on pegboard over the potting bench. Pots and seed flats not in use are stored clean, stacked according to size.

Zelma's greenhouse, like the basement, gradually filled up, and then the breezeway between the house and the garage was glassed in to form an all-year garden room. Now she is widely known as an authority on growing plants from seeds. With the companionship of plants, she has turned retirement into her crowning glory.

Many retired people are denied Zelma's kind of independence. At the Rossmoor community for senior citizens just outside Princeton, New Jersey, where I have lectured, there is an active garden club of several hundred members. On one occasion I demonstrated how to plant several different kinds of bowl gardens. Members who wished to put into practice their interpretation of what they had seen me demonstrate could sign up for their own planting session two weeks later. The outdoor gardens belonging to the individual residents of Rossmoor, although not large in square feet, are beautifully maintained, most of them a carefully chosen collection of favorite flowers from previous homes.

Rossmoor is fairly typical of this kind of development for senior citizens. Some also have a sizable community greenhouse as well as land set aside for vegetable gardening, with each resident entitled to a plot of ground measuring perhaps twenty by twenty feet in which to grow vegetables, herbs, and annuals.

High-rise apartments for senior citizens do not always have the land for individual or community gardens. In these situations house plants are the answer, and when natural light is not strong enough, fluorescent-light gardens are an increasingly popular substitute.

Of major importance is a pilot program called "Happiness Gardening," developed by the Men's Garden Club of Rockford, Illinois, in cooperation with the Men's Garden Clubs of America. C. Hal Nelson writes, "The MGCA has embarked on a new program in a field hitherto untouched by other garden and horticultural groups. It is happiness therapy through gardening for senior citizens."

That the idea works has been proven to the satisfaction of the members and also to the United States Department of Agriculture and Department of Housing and Urban Development. Nelson continues:

The idea was to finance and provide facilities and know-how for a gardening-under-lights program for the community's 350 senior citizens who live in federally financed high-rise apartments.

Richard Beck, an ardent garden clubber and a strong advocate of community service, originated the idea, which he took to the club president, who in turn won approval from the board of directors. Later the entire membership voted to allocate $700 to buy and build the necessary lights, tables, and materials and to install the equipment in a room in each of three Rockford high-rises.

Attendance at the weekly classes ranged from 50 to 80 persons. Beck and other members of the Rockford Men's Garden Club were responsible for each session, which lasted from one to two hours. "To get the program off to a fast start last year," Beck explained, "we wanted to get immediate blooms. So we planted slips from coleus, impatiens, and browallia. Later, miniature-tree seeds were planted to be used in a study of the art of bonsai in the second year. Next terrariums were made in small goldfish bowls. This was the most popular project."

Later, flower seeds were planted, and when spring came the seedlings were moved outdoors to supplement the plantings of professional gardeners. In all, thirty-five types of seeds and cuttings were used in the first year's program.

Interest remained high throughout the twenty-five weeks. Among the students were two in wheelchairs who were apologetic about taking up so much room. The plant room originally had been planned as a sewing center when the structure was built. In one high-rise it was necessary to crowd the plants into the laundry room. The students spend as much time as they wish. working with their own plants outside of the classes.

The senior citizen students do all the work themselves. After being shown how, each makes cuttings, plants seeds, and transplants, having first mixed the necessary potting soil.

The grass-roots "happiness gardening" program of the Rockford Men's Garden Club has been so successful that it is being adopted by other groups across the country. A complete outline entitled "Indoor Gardening for High-rise Apartments," which includes precisely detailed projects for twenty-five weeks, has been published by the Men's Garden Clubs of America, 5560 Merle Hay Road, Des Moines, Iowa 50323; the charge for a single copy is $10.

Volunteer and professional horticultural therapists are also hard at work expanding programs for the elderly and other people confined in institutions; this work is discussed further in Chapter 9.

6 ❧ Plants and Creativity

The world of plants offers an endless source of materials to satisfy the urge to be creative. Unfortunately, we have come to use the word creative to describe a certain type person, almost as if people can be divided as sheep and goats, into creative or noncreative. I maintain that we all have a natural urge to be creative, and that to deny the urge is to breed frustration and feelings of inadequacy.

Almost everywhere we turn in a garden, whether indoors or outdoors, there is opportunity to be creative. Matching a plant to a container that uniquely suits it from both a cultural and an esthetic viewpoint is to be creative. Arranging the rows in a vegetable garden so as to have the lowest growers toward the south, progressing upward to the tallest—probably corn—on the north assures maximum sunlight for all; arranging within this framework to contrast green-leaf lettuce with the bronzy oak-leaf variety, or to contrast the round heads of cabbage with the verticality of onions is to be creative.

Some people do this intuitively, others do it consciously. An awareness of the possibilities will help you be consciously creative; then as you develop confidence in yourself as a creative gardener, natural intuition will begin to take over. You may find that you are more creative than you or your parents, teachers, and friends ever thought you were.

Charles Webster, president of the Horticultural Society of New York, believes that plants are one of the greatest creative life forces we have. "Plants know how to use solar energy—we don't. Color, scent, and symmetry are beautiful and satisfying to man. Each plant has a personality. Plants and gardening are especially good when you need quiet time by yourself; they offer a combination of relaxation and learning."

Bonsai, espalier, and topiary, the gardening forms suggested in this chapter, are highly creative. In addition, they tend to be demanding, not in the sense of hard work but in the need for frequent watering, pruning, staking, tying, and training in general. They are not projects you can start and finish in a day, but rather living art forms that need almost daily attentions over long periods of time.

In bonsai, the Japanese art of dwarfing woody plant materials, a tree several hundred years old that in nature might tower a hundred feet tall can be maintained at a height of two or three feet with the roots anchored in a shallow bowl or tray holding perhaps less than a gallon of earth.

As practiced originally bonsai were quite naturally trees and shrubs indigenous to the local climate, which happened to be temperate, and therefore the plant materials were cold-hardy types that not only survive but need an annual period of dormancy induced by winter freezing.

Our friendly involvement with Japan since World War II has given us such a wide-ranging awareness of bonsai that it has become a major American pastime. The basic shapes and techniques used to nurture bonsai remain pure Japanese, but the range of plant materials has been vastly expanded. Most important is the use of small-leaved tropical trees and shrubs that do not require, in fact could not survive, a period of dormancy. This makes the cultivation of bonsai possible whether or not you have an outdoor garden. Natural light is not a requisite either; countless tropicals are suited to cultivation as bonsai in a fluorescent-light garden.

The specific how-to of bonsai is covered in many popular books. There are also national bonsai societies with many local branches; the addresses are included in Chapter 8. Apart from choosing the right plant materials to work with, bonsai requires a long-range commitment to thoughtful, careful pruning and shaping as well as unswerving faithfulness to watering. Bonsai is generally not suited to the absentee gardener, the person who for reasons of business or pleasure is frequently away from home for extended periods of time. For almost anyone else it can be a source of great satisfaction. Bonsai, probably more than any other gardening practice, requires a sensitivity to the plant's needs and appearance for an indefinite period, the potential being a lifetime of involvement between a plant and a person. This has been likened by some to transcendental meditation, or a positive way of forgetting everything. If the plant chosen for training is by nature long-lived, and it never suffers debilitating neglect, the bonsai can be passed along from one generation to the next as a living family heirloom.

Although a well-grown bonsai is a work of art to which almost everyone responds, the techniques used to achieve the effect may seem cruel to the person who is not involved in growing plants. Bonsai artists wrap branches with wire to hold them in desired angles and positions. The wires are not removed until the branches, through natural growth, can assume their assigned poses willingly. Interestingly enough, however, bonsai often captures the interest of individuals who have never gardened before.

One of my friends who grows and collects bonsai is Gene Boucher, a baritone with the Metropolitan Opera, who was first introduced to the art while on tour in Japan. "I had always been a gardener," he says, "but this highly developed art form appealed to me as a way of establishing a deeper involvement with individual plants. Since I travel frequently, bonsai is not something I could practice were it not for a devoted friend who shares my appreciation for the little trees and shrubs and gladly accepts the responsibility for their care when I am away."

One of the most remarkable private collections of bonsai in the United States is that of Ernesta and Frederic L. Ballard. Although Ernesta is one of America's foremost gardeners and a prominent figure in horticultural circles, Fred's involvement for many years was only to the extent of being a cheerful and willing helper. When Ernesta began to train some plants as bonsai, Fred realized that his interest in them was greater than helping to mix the potting soil or to apply water twice a day in summer. In just a few years the Philadelphia lawyer who once attended horticultural meetings primarily as the husband of Ernesta Ballard has become one of the country's leading experts in the art of nurturing bonsai.

Part of the charm and beauty of a bonsai lies in selecting a container uniquely suited in size, shape, and color to that of the plant. Finding the containers is a pleasant diversion, and something the Ballards and Boucher find gives a special focus to their travels. There is always some out-of-the-way nursery or antique shop to look up, and there possibly discover a beautiful container to carry home and find its perfect match in a plant.

An awareness of what makes a bonsai truly beautiful has made the Ballards better gardeners generally, they say. The trees around their property, many of which tower well over a hundred feet tall, have been pruned to emphasize their majesty. Soil has been carefully pulled away from the bases, just enough to reveal the tops of the large roots that buttress the giant trunks. Velvety moss carpets the ground between. Even ordinary house plants cultivated by the Ballards become extraordinary when planted in decorative pots or other containers whose color and shape provide a subtle complement to the leaves, flowers, and stems.

Espaliering is a garden art form which originated in Europe, not so much to be artistic as to train fruit trees against a south-facing wall in order to lengthen the growing season and to assure a crop in climates where it might not have been possible otherwise. An espaliered plant is two-dimensional; it has height and width but relatively little depth.

Because the gardeners who originated the practice of espaliering were creative, consciously or instinctively, standard patterns developed as highly stylized tree shapes or geometric patterns. In time ornamental plants came to be used in these decorative espalier patterns. In this country they are being used more and more, especially in the company of contemporary architecture, which often provides a span of unbroken wall space that can be used as a sort of canvas on which to attach and train the espalier. Among shrubs, pyracantha, euonymus, cotoneaster, forsythia, and viburnum are relatively easy to espalier.

House plants are seldom considered subjects for espaliering, but by the use of hardware cloth or redwood frames it is possible to train many of them. I have found great pleasure in training scented geraniums such as Old Scarlet Unique into decorative espalier patterns, as well as coleus, hoya, crown of thorns, shrimp plant, myrtle, rosemary, cestrum, and Chinese hibiscus.

Until I edited a book about espaliering I was only vaguely aware of the practice. Then, with my consciousness raised, I began to notice espaliers in many gardens, both public and private.

Either my ignorance kept me from appreciating them before, or more American gardeners began to cultivate them at about that time.

In my pre–New York outdoor garden I planted three established apple-tree espaliers along the redwood fence that served as the backdrop for the flower border. Keeping the branches tied in place, nipping back tips to encourage fullness, and pruning out unwanted excess growth was something I always enjoyed. It took about as long to groom one of the espaliers as it takes for me to shower and shave in the morning.

My neighbor at the time had a chain-link fence that ran at right angles to my redwood, and although it kept his dogs out of my garden it was an eyesore. Then I hit upon the idea of planting young forsythia bushes all along the chain-link and training them in various classic espalier patterns. My neighbor not only liked my idea but offered to keep the lawn grass edged and trimmed on either side if I would maintain the espaliers. The chain-link was a perfect support for espalier work, since its gridwork provided a secure place to tie a branch wherever I needed to. Forsythia grows so rapidly that by the end of the first season all the patterns were established. The following spring every line of the designs was a ribbon of yellow bloom, and by the end of summer the espaliers were complete.

That same season I planted pyracanthas in an espalier pattern along the blank wall of the garage, which had been an annoyance as part of the garden view. Within a few weeks the espalier began to take shape, and by autumn the foliage presented a handsome, distinctive design; the bright orange-red pyracantha berries were beautiful and lasted well into the winter.

The following summer I discovered still another application of the espalier technique: I trained Big Boy tomato plants up the narrow wall space on either side of the double-garage door, which faced the west. They grew rapidly and proved easy subjects to espalier. By August the stems reached the eaves of the house. The warmth of the wall and my constant removal of unwanted suckers yielded the biggest crop of tomatoes I have ever harvested from two plants.

Books about espaliering are not as plentiful as those about bonsai. Espalier is discussed in many general gardening books, but the only thorough treatment I know, with reference to house plants in particular, is in *The Art of Training Plants,* by Ernesta Drinker Ballard.

Topiary is the art of training plants into various animal or geometric shapes—a seal, a dog, a peacock, a human being, an obelisk, a sphere, a pyramid. Perhaps most familiar is the practice of training a normally bushy or shrublike plant into a tree. A tree rose is in itself a form of topiary, but one that requires relatively complicated grafting techniques.

It is not difficult to train a geranium, coleus, lantana, or Chinese hibiscus into a standard or topiary tree. Start with a strong, rooted, unbranched cutting. Insert a sturdy wood or bamboo stake in the pot alongside the cutting, of a length equal to the height of the trunk you would like your tree to have. Then use a plant tie to attach the stem of the cutting to the stake every few inches. Pinch out all branches that begin to form, thus directing the plant's strength into growing the one main stem taller and taller until it reaches the top of the stake. At this point pinch out the growing tip to encourage branching. When the resulting branches are two or three inches long, pinch out the tips of each. Continue this procedure until the head of the tree is rounded and full. Meanwhile you can begin to remove the foliage that grows along the trunk, finally leaving a bare, straight trunk attached to the stake, crowned by a head of foliage and flowers.

Topiaries shaped as animals or geometrics are often based on a galvanized wire form that may be stuffed with moistened sphagnum moss into which short, rooted cuttings are planted; small-leaved English ivy is a popular choice. The plants are wired and pruned to cover the form completely. Making the forms is part of the fun, and it can be a cooperative venture. Animal forms may be grand or whimsical, depending on your taste and that of those who share your garden. Specific projects and how-to details are included in the Ballard book, *The Art of Training Plants*.

Other garden art forms include terrariums; bottle gardens; miniature landscapes created in a dish, bowl, or tray; underwater gardens of aquarium plants; and vivariums that combine plants and pets. All these are illustrated and described in many popular books. Collections of naturally small or slow-growing plants grouped together as a miniature landscape or garden are especially rewarding for any person who is confined indoors. These may be cultivated in natural or artificial light, and the care of such a garden, perhaps using manicure scissors instead of pruning shears and a kitchen fork instead of a garden rake or spade for cultivating, can occupy many hours in pleasant, productive activity that requires relatively little mobility or strength.

7 ❦ Plants and Children

As a child, I sometimes thought it was strange for me to care as much about plants as I did. Now I realize that I was lucky. An involvement with plants teaches responsibility, consideration for something living, the rewards of being patient—psychologists call it delayed gratification—and generally helps establish a feeling for how the natural world works.

The earlier a child learns that plants live in cycles, some for only one season (annuals), some for two (biennials), and some for much longer periods of time (perennials, including trees and shrubs), the greater will be his or her understanding of life itself. I grew up keenly aware of seasonal changes, beginnings and endings, natural highs and lows, and this foundation is an invaluable aid to emotional well-being.

Another individual who believes that children need to grow up in the company of plants is Robert Steffen, the farm manager for Father Flanagan's Boys' Home in Boys Town, Nebraska. Upon learning of my work on this book, he wrote:

79

I have always felt that all people, but especially the young, need to understand their relationship to the earth in order for them to really become well-adjusted, mature, and balanced individuals. One cannot begin to understand this relationship without knowing something about living plants and animals.

During thirty years as farm manager here I have seen many a boy who came trusting no one, including himself, and communicating with no one. Then he becomes attached to a small calf that he feeds, and thus begins to look at things from a different perspective and to gain some self-confidence. Or seeds he plants in the vegetable garden produce something to be eaten and shared.

Generally the farm and gardens have been looked upon as places where boys could learn how to work. They desperately need this, probably more today than ever. Many young people simply don't know how to do much of anything. Nor have very many of them ever really been exposed to living things, whether they be plants or animals. Common sense has become a rare commodity. It is because of this that I feel an involvement with plants and animals may be one of youth's greatest needs today. For that matter, our society generally has lost touch with the living world and thus has alienated itself from the earth and brought to the fore what we are calling the environmental crisis. We have lost respect for life.

Gardening is good therapy for young and old. The earth has great healing power. It is the plant of course which makes it all possible. Simply realizing that we could not exist on this planet without the plant should be significant. Learning how and why this is true can occupy much of a lifetime and be only a beginning. Plants are miraculous creations. They hold so many secrets that they present a challenge and a hope for men of all ages, rich and poor, learned and the not so learned. Plants are indeed a source of great hope for our time and for the many people who are disturbed, frustrated, and concerned about the future. Knowing and understanding plants can give them hope and reassurance that with death there follows life and the great cycles of the seasons are part of even greater rhythms of the universe that are not dependent on mortal man's manipulation.

My first gardening experience was something I shared with someone I loved, my mother. And gardening is such a natural, vital part of life that it should be something we share with others whom we love. The more I realize the positive effects of plants on people, the more therapeutic the act of sharing is for me.

Little children respond to almost anything that grows, but they are not long on patience. Something quick, like a navy bean, makes a good beginning. The sensitive plant (*Mimosa pudica*) whose leaves fold up right before your eyes when you touch them is a sure winner. Cuttings that root quickly and dependably in a glass of water are a lot of fun and needn't cost anything—unless you have to buy pots and potting soil when the roots are about an inch long and ready for a permanent home. Coleus, Swedish ivy, and wandering Jew are great plants for projects like this.

The school classroom is an obvious place to teach gardening, and I have been doing it off and on for the ten years since my oldest child, Mark, became a first-grader. My urban children and their friends are vastly more aware of the necessity of plants for survival than even the country classmates of my childhood were.

Last year I taught Jeannene's fifth-grade class of some thirty-five pupils about gardening, making a one-hour visit each week through the spring months. Our goal was for each child to plant a cutting and grow it to the point of producing something salable for the annual P-TA fund-raising bazaar.

Rather than do the talking first and the planting later, I chose to start with cuttings I had taken from my own plants. While the teacher kept the rest of the class occupied, I worked with

five children at a time, showing them how to mix their own potting soil and how to plant the cutting. (We used approximately
equal parts of vermiculite and packaged all-purpose potting
soil; the vermiculite was to encourage rapid rooting and the soil
to sustain growth thereafter.) We then labeled each pot, including the Latin and common name of the plant, the date of
planting, and the child's name.

After all the children had planted cuttings, I spoke to the entire class, summarizing what we had just done. I explained the
meanings of the Latin names and why it is important to use
them if you want to communicate exactly what plant you have
in mind, since common names vary widely from place to place.
Swedish ivy was one of the plants we had been working with,
and because it is neither from Sweden nor a true ivy, the Latin
name, *Plectranthus australis,* was obviously meaningful. After I
had written it out on the blackboard I asked the students what
they thought the name meant. At least half of them guessed
that Swedish ivy came from Australia, which is correct. *Nauti-
localyx forgetii* was not so easily translated, but after I explained it the children loved the name. The flowers of this gesneriad (related to the African violet) are borne in a boat-shaped
calyx and the plant was discovered by a man whose name was
Forget.

The next day Jeannene told me that some of the cuttings had
wilted, so I sent a roll of plastic bags to school with her and she
shared with her classmates what I had showed her how to do:
first check the soil to see that there is enough moisture, then enclose the cutting and the top of the pot in the plastic bag and
secure the miniature greenhouse with a rubber band. They did
this first thing that morning, and as soon as Jeannene got home
from school she called me excitedly to say that all the leaves
had perked up by lunchtime.

The following week I gave the children a lesson on how to

pinch the tip out of a young plant to encourage it to form more branches. And we talked about how much and how often potted plants need water and fertilizer.

Another time we planted Tiny Tim tomato seeds in Jiffy Seven pellets, which are compressed peat moss surrounded by fine netting. Five minutes after one of these pellets, which is about the size of a silver dollar and a fourth of an inch thick, is dropped into a container of water, it swells to two inches tall and is ready to use for planting seeds or small cuttings. A week later most of the tomato seeds had germinated, and we were ready to talk about what had happened, future care of the young seedlings, and how each child would be able to take the tomato plants home at the end of school and grow them through the summer in a sunny window, on an apartment terrace, or outdoors in the country.

At one of the weekly sessions with Jeannene's class I brought along about a dozen miniature plants which we used to create a Lilliputian landscape inside a large, empty fish tank that had been found in one of the school storage closets. This time we had not only the individual plants to discuss but their relationship in the terrarium, which represented a microcosm of nature.

I never left one of these hour-long periods of sharing without feeling tremendously rewarded. At some point I told the children that the cuttings they had planted would eventually become potbound and would need to be moved to larger pots. Perhaps what pleased me most about the whole experience was the day when Jeannene brought her coleus plant to me and said, "Dad, it's potbound. Could you show me how to repot it?"

I realize now that I made a mistake in my earlier efforts to garden with my own children. I tried to help them plant entire gardens out of doors. They were excited over digging up the soil, opening the colorful packets, and planting the seeds. But I never could rekindle enough of this excitement to get them to assume responsibility for what sprouted and grew in the garden. My plans were much too ambitious for their short spans of attention.

Now my children are older; this year Mark will be sixteen, Steven fifteen, and Jeannene twelve. Instead of becoming those rotten teenagers people—and unfortunately some parents—talk about, they have grown up to be my friends. This has strengthened the traditional parent-child relationship to such an extent that we are what the children call up-front with each other. Part of this close, open feeling is rooted in the way we garden together outdoors in warm weather and indoors all year.

Mark is the chief electrician, always ready to wire up another fluorescent-light garden for me. At one point we had so many plants that he suggested hanging a fixture with two 20-watt tubes under a skirted table. This took advantage of wasted space, the floor-length cloth helped maintain humidity for the plants, and the light inside made the cloth glow at night. Gardening teaches resourcefulness and adaptability, both requisites for living well.

Outdoors, Mark likes to clear away brush, drive a garden tractor to mow the lawn, and do heavy work in general. He spends part of each summer helping my father farm in Oklahoma, and is considering some branch of agriculture as a career.

Steven and Jeannene are decidedly more interested in house plants, and each is well into collecting and filling their bedroom windows with cuttings I give them to root. Jeannene regularly adopts any of Steven's ailing plants and takes pride in nursing them back to health. When asked about her career interests she has always said she wants to be a doctor; will she become a plant physiologist or horticultural therapist? Steven's inclinations are toward art and the theater; he might grow up to be a producer, director, set designer, or playwright who insists that live plants and flowers play a role on stage as well as off.

Although formal horticultural therapy programs are discussed in Chapter 9, you don't necessarily have to go that far to share your love of gardening with a child or a group of children. What it takes to have a classroom gardening project is one dedicated person who is good at organization. Being a gardener is no prerequisite, although it helps. The classroom may be your own—as student or teacher, or indirectly as a parent—or you can offer your services to a school simply as a concerned outsider.

If you need funding for pots, soil, and fertilizer, it may be available from the school (doubtful) or the P-TA (more likely). An appeal to the classroom parents may yield the necessary contributions if you outline your plan and objectives convincingly. Local nurserymen, florists, and garden-center owners may also be interested to the extent of helping with supplies.

Acquiring plant materials should never be a problem, because parents and children of the class are almost always able to donate enough cuttings for all to share. One good-sized hanging basket of Swedish ivy or wandering Jew may well yield up to a hundred cuttings—and grow all the better for having been thinned and shared.

8 ❧ Friends Through Plants

One sure way to make new friends who share a common interest is to adopt one particular kind of plant for which there is a national society and join it. I was ten years old when I first found the address of the Amercan Begonia Society and sent off my application for membership.

I was soon receiving the Society's monthly publication, *The Begonian,* participating in round-robin correspondence, writing letters to individual members (I had by now swapped a steer for a typewriter), exchanging cuttings by mail, and buying rare seeds for a nominal price from a seed fund maintained by and for the members. My collection of begonias grew rapidly, I became a better grower, and hardly a day passed that I did not find in our mailbox friendly letters from fellow ABS members.

At about this time *Flower Grower* and *Popular Gardening* magazines began to publish reports of some extraordinary hybrid gloxinias being developed by an American breeder, Albert Buell. Coincidentally, one of my begonia pen pals had earlier found Buell's offer of hybrid gloxinia seeds in a classified advertisement and not only had grown the seeds she purchased to flowering size but had done some cross-pollinating herself. Gloxinias set seeds with relative ease, and before long my friend had more than she knew what to do with. She sent me hundreds of seeds and a whole bag of tubers that had formed from her first batch of seedlings.

I figured that in no time my new lean-to greenhouse would be filled with the velvety trumpet- or slipper-shaped gloxinia flowers. But success did not come easily. If the tiny seeds sprouted, excessive heat withered them away, and although the tubers produced plenty of healthy foliage, the flower buds that formed built up my hopes only to disappoint me by turning brown before they were much bigger than a pea. I shared all this with my pen pals and received a lot of friendly advice and sympathy.

In early January of 1951 we had a blizzard that kept us snowbound for the better part of two weeks. I had nothing to do except putter with my plants and reread all my magazines. Then the idea occurred to me, if there was a begonia society, why shouldn't there be a gloxinia society? I sent off a letter to this effect to the editor of *Flower Grower* magazine and it was published in the March issue. In response to my suggestion that persons interested in forming such an organization write to me I received several hundred letters. Perhaps the most important of these was from a Mrs. Kathryn M. Schulz of Minneapolis, dated May 27, 1951:

Dear Elvin McDonald: I read your request in *Flower Grower*. I'm sure that you will have enough answers to flood your place. I've longed for just such a society. I have been interested in the Gesneria Family [to which gloxinias belong] for some time now. Information is mighty scarce on these lovely things. I've been gathering explanatory data to do an article on them for *Flower Grower* and have had very little help.

My specimens are small but I love them. Here's what I have and what I've been promised: *Kohleria picta, K. hirsuta, Gesneria cardinalis, Hypocratum mummelaria, Gloxinia maculata,* Brazilian gloxinia, corytholoma, achimenes, didymocarpus, and episcias.

Gloxinia maculata is only a promise. I had *Hypocratum mummelaria* but lost it. The trouble is when you don't have a greenhouse to work with, there just doesn't seem to be any one to help you with the soil typings and diseases.

I would love to be in on the ground floor of such a movement. I hope I can get together enough blooming specimen pictures to make a good article. That will further the cause and push us further toward a society.

I replied immediately, telling Mrs. Schulz that I was a fourteen-year-old farm boy and inviting her to serve as co-editor of what was about to become *The Gloxinian,* publication of the about-to-be American Gloxinia Society.

Although the letter I received from her in response is not dated, I am sure it came by return mail. It began, "Dear Elvin: Call me Peggie after this, it simplifies things." I had planned a monthly magazine, the same as *The Begonian,* but Peggie wisely advised, "Why not have it bimonthly until you get started? You will be busier than you ever dreamed, and most new publications, even under the experienced hand of an old editor, come out this way." I took her advice, and with a manuscript Peggie sent to me about gloxinias and their relatives, the gesneriads, and an article by Albert Buell on how to grow gloxinias, I began to formulate the first issue. Other growers who responded to my letter had offered material for publication, and before long I had more than enough to make up a twelve-page bulletin. Enough people had sent membership dues so that when someone suggested a good but cheap printer somewhere in Kansas, I did the necessary correspondence and soon a bundle of manuscripts and photographs was on its way.

Of course I will never forget the day that first issue of *The Gloxinian* arrived. I was plowing a dry, dusty field of wheat stubble some distance from the house. My mother came driving into the field at noontime to bring me my lunch, but more important, she had a carton of magazines waiting for me in the back seat. The experience was so satisfying that I was to become an editor for life.

Within a few months we had several hundred members, and before long there were several thousand. The mail arrived in bundles, the volume increasing eventually to the point of changing our little post office from a lowly three or four rating to a number one. Mrs. Kerns, the postmistress, loved me because her salary increased with each change of classification. We had fun, too, as she and my mother helped me place the magazines in addressed envelopes once every two months, then sort them by state and city, tying, weighing, and bagging them so they could be sent on their way—all over the United States and to many foreign countries.

Until the volume of correspondence overwhelmed me, I kept all of this a secret from my friends. I had one life that I maintained by mail and a whole other life very much like that of my school and church friends. But eventually I couldn't cope with answering all the letters about membership in the society, so I began to hire my school friends to help me on Saturdays. At times there would be as many as five or six sitting around our big dining table, one or two typing, the others stuffing envelopes or alphabetizing mailing lists. I had a sort of pact with them that they would not discuss any of this because I didn't want to be ostracized by the kids who knew me less well at school.

Eventually my father's pride in what I was doing got the best of him and he showed *The Gloxinian* to the school superintendent, who promptly revealed what I was doing to the entire faculty and student body. I got kidded a little, but mostly I was treated as a hero.

The word about me spread and I began to be in demand for lectures and radio and television appearances; garden editors of major magazines asked me to write feature articles on how to grow gloxinias. Fortunately, by this time I had learned how to overcome the environmental difficulties of the lean-to and the gloxinias were blooming as freely as the African violets I had once found difficult.

Through all this my parents were supportive but treated me no differently from before. Meanwhile, I had many mentors who began to council me about my future, how I should be educated and where. Peggie Schulz, who by this time had achieved a certain fame in her own right, having written a popular book called *Gloxinias and How to Grow Them,* treated me as her equal. We shared plant experiences, problems and plans for the society. My voice and piano teacher took it upon herself to lecture me weekly not to marry in high school, as was fairly common among my peers, and Fay Scott Payne, who lived about a hundred miles away, in Enid, Oklahoma, whipped my manners into shape ("Three quiet stirs is sufficient to dissolve the sugar in your iced tea") so that I would not make a fool of myself in public. Another society member, Paul Arnold, then president of Ansco Films, made me understand the importance of spelling plant names correctly and using the correct names so as not to contribute to existing confusion. And Bill Coates, who among other things developed the recipe for Fritos, impressed on me the value of establishing career goals for myself in the field of journalism.

Meanwhile, the American Gloxinia Society joined the American Horticultural Society, and I, being the chief officer, albeit self-appointed, represented the AGS at meetings of the AHS. This responsibility took me by train and plane to Boston, where at age sixteen I finally met the editors with whom I had been corresponding. They discussed story ideas with me, gave me writing assignments, made sure I had Cokes to drink with them in the informal meetings they carried on in the bar, and got me off to bed at a reasonable hour. Mrs. Victor Ries, whose husband was a distinguished professor of horticulture at Ohio State University, took me to hear the Boston Symphony on a Saturday afternoon. It was my first brush with real culture.

I returned to Oklahoma having fallen in love with the reality of a world I had known only through the printed words I sent and received from our R.F.D. mailbox. In a few years my involvement with the gloxinia had changed my life, as I was to see the gloxinia change many other lives later on.

In particular I think of those two couples whose marriages were enriched if not saved by gloxinias, and of Albert Buell, Mr. Gloxinia himself, who met his wife, Diantha, through the American Gloxinia Society (now the American Gloxinia and Gesneriad Society).

Obviously you don't need to wait until a relationship is slipping before you think about what fun you might have gardening together, and you don't need to be looking for a spouse. The plant societies for which I have listed addresses at the end of this chapter are filled with friends and couples who share an interest in one particular kind of plant, which serves as a focus for day-to-day living as well as vacations and travel to meet fellow members and growers. Most of the societies publish an annual membership roster so that by means of correspondence or telephoning you can plan your travels and visits accordingly.

Plant societies also have branch chapters in major cities and some not so major; you may be able to participate in local meetings where you will not only make friends but be able to learn the finer points of growing your chosen plant, exchange experiences and problems with others, and new species and varieties. The societies also sponsor local and national competitive flower shows and sometimes organize tours to various parts of the world to visit beautiful private and public gardens as well as famous nurseries and plant breeders.

Gardeners have always seemed to me a universally friendly people, eager to share experiences and plants. I have found that a genuine interest in plants can bridge more communications gaps than almost anything else. A classic example of this happened recently in the life of one of my friends, who is in every way the image the world expects of a trend-setting fashion plate. Underneath all this glamour she is one of the most serious and dedicated plant people I have ever known. At times her looks have put off professional greenhouse growers who took for granted that no one who looked like that could possibly know the difference between a leaf and a petal.

Then she hit upon the answer: Drop a few Latin names when you feel the cold shoulder.

I came to this realization when I walked into an ancient greenhouse in the country. I saw nothing when I walked through the door except the best Boston fern I had ever seen. So I said out loud what I was thinking: "Where on earth did you get that magnificent *Nephrolepis exaltata bostoniensis?*" By the time I had all of that enunciated, the owner, who looked even more ancient than the greenhouse, had tears in his eyes as he said, "Do you know, this is the first time in my life anyone has ever walked in and called that plant anything other than Boston fern."

My friend and the old man spent the better part of the afternoon together. He showed her rare plants tucked here and there that the average visitor would have never seen.

An interest in plants can transcend the communications gaps of class distinction, race, level of education, and even language, since the Latin names for plants are always the same no matter where you find them. I once spent a morning in Milan looking at color plates of plants. The printer thoughtfully provided me with a translator who spoke both Italian and English, to help me communicate with the curator of the plates, who spoke only Italian. Right away we were all laughing together because I would ask to see something like *Sinningia* and the translator would formulate my question in Italian using the same key word, *"Sinningia."* The plate keeper and I communicated the rest of the morning without difficulty—and without the translator.

If the plant of your choice is not included in any of the societies listed here, maybe you will become the founder of a society, as I did for the gloxinia, helped to do for the geranium, and tried without much success for the miniature rose. (In retrospect I realize I was ahead of my time, or rather the miniature rose's; I suspect today's interest could easily sustain such an organization.)

In the list you will find the name and address of each society listed alphabetically by plant or specialty, followed by an indication of local chapters if they exist and the name and frequency of the organization's publications. The costs of membership have not been included because they change from time to time, but most dues are less than $10 per year. When you write to ask for information about joining a plant society, it will help speed a reply if you enclose with your request a large-size, stamped, self-addressed envelope.

Plant Societies and Periodicals

American Begonia Society, Inc.
139 North Ledoux Road
Beverly Hills, California 90211
The Begonian

Bonsai Clubs International
445 Blake Street
Menlo Park, California 94025

The American Bonsai Society
953 South Shore Drive
Lake Waukomis
Parksville, Missouri 64151
Bonsai (quarterly)
ABStracts (interim monthly newsletter)

The Bonsai Society of Greater New York, Inc.
Box E, Bronx Park
Bronx, New York 10466
The Bonsai Bulletin (quarterly)

Bonsai Society of Texas
Box 11054
Dallas, Texas 75235

The American Boxwood Society
Box 85
Boyce, Virginia 22620
The Boxwood Bulletin (quarterly)

Bromeliad Society, Inc.
P.O. Box 3279
Santa Monica, California 90403
Regional chapters in the South and New York
The Bromeliad Journal (6 times per year)

Cactus and Succulent Society of America, Inc.
Box 167
Reseda, California 91335
Cactus and Succulent Journal (bi-monthly)

California Native Plant Society
Suite 317
2490 Channing Way
Berkeley, California 94704

The American Camellia Society
Box 212
Fort Valley, Georgia 31030
85 local, state or regional chapters
The Camellia Journal

National Chrysanthemum Society, Inc., U.S.A.
394 Central Avenue
Mountainside, New Jersey 07092
NCS Journal,
The Chrysanthemum (quarterly) plus a show issue in January

Cymbidium Society of America, Inc.
6787 Worsham Drive
Whittier, California 90602
2 branch chapters
Cymbidium Society News

The American Daffodil Society, Inc.
89 Chichester Road
New Canaan, Connecticut 06840
9 Regions represented by Directors
The Daffodil Journal (quarterly)

The American Dahlia Society
163 Grant Street
Dover, New Jersey 07801
75 societies throughout U.S.A.
ADS bulletin (quarterly)

The Delphinium Society
7540 Ridgeway Road
Minneapolis, Minnesota 55426
Yearbook

Elm Research Institute
Harrisville, New Hampshire 03450

Epiphyllum Society of America
218 East Greystone Avenue
Monrovia, California 91016
Epiphyllum Bulletin (irregular)

American Fern Society
Biological Sciences Group
University of Connecticut
Storrs, Connecticut 06268
American Fern Journal (quarterly)

Los Angeles International Fern Society
2423 Burritt Avenue
Redondo Beach, California 90278
Newsletter and annual magazine

Flower and Garden Magazine
4251 Pennsylvania Avenue
Kansas City, Missouri 64111
Monthly magazine. Gardening indoors/outdoors.

Dwarf Fruit Trees Assn.
Department of Horticulture
Michigan State University
East Lansing, Michigan 48823
Compact Fruit Trees (bimonthly)
Compact Composit (proceedings of annual conference)

The American Fuchsia Society
Hall of Flowers
Golden Gate Park
San Francisco, California 94122

National Fuchsia Society
10934 East Flory Street
Whittier, California 90606
The National Fuchsia Fan (monthly)

International Geranium Society
11960 Pascal Avenue
Colton, California 92324
5 regional chapters
Geraniums Around the World (quarterly)

The American Gesneria Society
11983 Darlington Avenue
Los Angeles, California 90049
Gesneriad Saintpaulia News (bimonthly)

North American Gladiolus Council
30 Highland Place
Peru, Indiana 46970
NAGC Bulletin (quarterly)

The American Gloxinia/Gesneriad Society, Inc.
P.O. Box 174
New Milford, Connecticut 06776
The Gloxinian (bimonthly)

American Gourd Society
P.O. Box 274
Mount Gilead, Ohio 43338
The Gourd (3 times per year)

American Hemerocallis Society
Signal Mountain, Tennessee 37377
The American Hemerocallis Journal (quarterly)

The Herb Society of America
300 Massachusetts Avenue
Boston, Massachusetts 02115
1000 members; units in many states
The Herbarist (annually)

The American Hibiscus Society
Box 98
Eagle Lake, Florida 33139
Seed Pod (quarterly)

The Holly Society of America, Inc.
407 Fountain Green Road
Bel Air, Maryland 21014
Holly Letter (3 times per year)
Proceedings (once every two years)

The American Horticultural Society
River Farm
Mount Vernon, Virginia
News and Views newsletter six times yearly
American Horticulturist magazine six times yearly

Horticulture
300 Massachusetts Avenue
Boston, Massachusetts
Monthly magazine. Gardening indoors/outdoors

The American Hosta Society
114 The Fairway
Albert Lea, Minnesota 56007
The American Hosta Society Newsletter,
Bulletin of The American Hosta Society

The Indoor Light Gardening Society of America, Inc.
423 Powell Drive
Bay Village, Ohio 44140

The American Iris Society
2315 Tower Grove Avenue
St. Louis, Missouri 63110
24 regional societies
Bulletin of The American Iris Society

Median Iris Society
10 South Franklin Circle
Littleton, Colorado 80121
Section of American Iris Society
The Medianite (quarterly)

Reblooming Iris Society
903 Tyler Avenue
Radford, Virginia 24141
Reblooming Iris Recorder (tri-annually)

The Society for Japanese Irises
17225 McKenzie Highway, Rt. 2
Springfield, Oregon 97477
The American Iris Society (quarterly bulletins)
The Society for Japanese Irises (bulletins)

Society for Louisiana Irises
Box 175
University of SW Louisiana
Lafayette, Louisiana 70501
Members in 30 states and overseas
Newsletter (quarterly)

The Society for Siberian Irises
South Harpswell, Maine 04079

Spuria Iris Society
Route 2, Box 83
Purcell, Oklahoma 73080
Spuria Newsletter (quarterly)

American Ivy Society
128 West 58th Street
New York, New York 10019
American Ivy Society Bulletin

The North American Lily Society, Inc.
Route 1, Box 395
Colby, Wisconsin 54421
14 regional societies
Quarterly bulletin; Yearbook

National Oleander Society
5127 Avenue O1/2
Galveston, Texas 77550
National Oleander Society (annual)

American Orchid Society, Inc.
Botanical Museum of Harvard University
Cambridge, Massachusetts 02138
American Orchid Society Bulletin

Organic Gardening and Farming
Emmaus, Pennsylvania
Monthly magazine. Gardening organically, indoors/outdoors

The Palm Society
1320 South Venetian Way
Miami, Florida 33139
5 chapters
Princepes (quarterly)

American Peony Society
250 Interlachen Road
Hopkins, Minnesota 55343
American Peony Society Bulletin (quarterly)

The American Plant Life Society
The American Amaryllis Society Group
Box 150
La Jolla, California 92037
Plantlife-Amaryllis Yearbook (bulletin)

Plants Alive
1255 Portland Place

Boulder, Colorado 80302
Monthly magazine. Gardening indoors

Popular Gardening Indoors
383 Madison Avenue
New York, New York 10017
Quarterly magazine. Gardening in containers, indoors/outdoors

The American Primrose Society
7100 South West 209th
Beaverton, Oregon 97005
Quarterly of the American Primrose Society

American Rhododendron Society
2232 N.E. 78th Avenue
Portland, Oregon 97213
35 chapters
The Quarterly Bulletin of the American Rhododendron Society

American Rock Garden Society
Office of the Secretary
90 Pierpont Road
Waterbury, Connecticut 06705
Thirteen regional chapters
American Rock Garden Society Bulletin (quarterly)

American Rose Society
P.O. Box 30,000
Shreveport, Louisiana 71130
Many districts throughout U.S.A.
The American Rose (monthly)

Saintpaulia International
Box 10604
Knoxville, Tennessee 37919
Gesneriad Saintpaulia News (bimonthly)

African Violet Society of America, Inc.
Box 1326

Knoxville, Tennessee 37901
African Violet Magazine (five times per year)

New England Wild Flower Society, Inc.
Hemenway Road
Framingham, Massachusetts 01701
New England Wild Flower Notes

In addition to the plant societies, there are garden club associations that sponsor local groups and conservation organizations that can help you get involved with other people who are concerned about ecology and the survival of both animal and plant life on our planet.

The women who make up the Garden Club of America and the National Council of State Garden Clubs, along with the men in the Men's Garden Clubs of America, have become aggressive, if not militant, in helping our country grow better, through local beautification projects, sponsorship of horticultural therapy programs, and a wide-ranging involvement in activities aimed at preserving natural beauty and abolishing insidious ugliness, especially along our public streets and highways.

Garden Club Associations

Garden Club of America
598 Madison Avenue
New York, New York 10022
12,500 members; clubs in all states
The Garden Club of America Bulletin (five times per year)

Ikebana International
CPO Box 1262
Tokyo, Japan

Open membership; chapters in most states
Ikebana International Magazine (quarterly)

Men's Garden Clubs of America
5560 Merle Hay Road
Des Moines, Iowa 50323
The Gardener (bimonthly)

National Council of State Garden Clubs, Inc.
4401 Magnolia Avenue
St. Louis, Missouri 63110
State federations and local clubs
The National Gardener (bimonthly)

Conservation Organizations

National Audubon Society
950 Third Avenue
New York, New York 10022
Audubon Magazine

National Council of Conservation Districts
Box 855
League City, Texas 77573

National Onion Assn.
201-½ East Grand River Ave.
East Lansing, Michigan 48823

Friends of the Earth
529 Commercial Street
San Francisco, California 94111
Not Man Apart (monthly)

Council on Environmental Quality
722 Jackson Place, N.W.
Washington, D.C. 20006

The American Forestry Association
1319 18th Street, Northwest
Washington, D.C. 20036
American Forests (monthly)

The Nature Conservancy
Suite 800
1800 North Kent Street
Arlington, Virginia 22209

National Parks and Conservation Assn.
1701 18th Street, Northwest
Washington, D.C. 20009
National Parks and Conservation Magazine: The Environmental Journal (monthly)

Sierra Club
1050 Mills Tower
San Francisco, California 94104
Sierra Club Bulletin (10 issues/year)
National News Report (48 issues/year)

The Izaak Walton League of America
1326 Waukegan Rd.
Glenview, Illinois 60025
Outdoor America

The Wilderness Society
1901 Pennsylvania Avenue, N.W.
Washington, D.C. 20006
The Living Wilderness

The National Wildlife Federation
1412 16th Street, Northwest
Washington, D.C. 20036
Conservation News
Ranger Rick's Nature Magazine

Plant societies, garden clubs, and related nature organizations are filled with individuals whose lives have been enriched by an involvement with others who share a similar interest. I think of Millie Thompson, who has found begonias the answer to living a productive life even though she has chronic hypertension. Her interest began with one ordinary semperflorens begonia which her husband Ed suggested she might enjoy growing. Together they have built the largest private collection of begonias in the world, and Millie has written the most complete begonia material in the literature on that popular plant.

When I first moved to New York I invited members of the American Gloxinia and Gesneriad Society who lived nearby to come to my apartment to organize the Metropolitan New York Chapter of AGGS. I suppose twenty or twenty-five members came that afternoon, and the group now numbers several hundred with its own periodical, regular meetings, and exhibits of fine plants. What I remember most is that my invitation that day went to one member in Brooklyn who, it turned out, was as provincial as any person I have ever met. But her interest in gloxinias made her forget herself; she came that afternoon on what was her first visit to Manhattan and took her first ride in an elevator. You will understand why I maintain that plants have a positive power over people who become involved with them.

More recently a dear friend of mine has undergone a period of severe depression that required hospitalization at first, then therapy as an outpatient, and now weekly visits to her analyst, who has encouraged her to get out and make new friends. As she tells the story, "I didn't have trouble meeting new people through my group therapy sessions, but our most obvious interest in common was depression and other emotional problems. What turned this around for me was remembering how my mother filled the house with plants when my sister and I went off to college. I decided plants could give me an outlet and fill a void in my life."

The rest of her story is fairly predictable. She bought some plants, I gave her some cuttings. The next time she met someone in group therapy who she felt could be a friend, she invited her to visit on a Saturday afternoon when there was some dividing and repotting to be done. "Instead of discussing our anxieties and battles with depression, we talked about plants and how they grow. I gave her a couple of them. Now she's frequenting the neighborhood plant shops, looking for kinds that appeal to her. We're sharing cuttings and experiences centered in a growing interest instead of sitting around feeling unwanted and unloved. Neither of us feels hopeless any more."

9 ❧ Plant Therapists

Gardening has been used in the treatment of certain emotional and physical problems for nearly two hundred years, but horticultural therapy as we know it today did not come into general practice until the late 1950s. I became aware of what was happening when it was my good fortune to edit a book called *Therapy Through Horticulture,* by Donald P. Watson and Alice W. Burlingame, which was published in 1960. A few years later, at a meeting of the Garden Writers Association of America, I met Rhea R. McCandliss, a soft-spoken, gentle woman who excited all of us by sharing her experiences in developing the horticultural therapy program at the Menninger Clinic in Topeka, Kansas.

Ms. McCandliss describes a horticultural therapist as "one who uses the knowledge of plants and gardening, greenhouse and floristry skills as a tool to develop a relationship with a patient for the dual purpose of helping that patient with the problem of adjustment, and encouraging the patient to develop a broader interest in his or her surroundings as a result of increased knowledge of the plant world."

To this definition Ms. Burlingame adds, "In horticultural therapy you develop a program of working with flowers and plants, with the primary objective being to raise the level of motivation for the patient—whether his or her problem is mental or physical. Response will come from the patient in a renewed confidence, a warm feeling of achievement, and a greater interest in tomorrow than yesterday."

Basic to horticultural therapy is its tremendous adaptability. Work with plants, flowers, and gardens can be adjusted to every age, every illness or need. It has proven so beneficial that several universities (listed at the end of this chapter) now offer degrees in horticultural therapy.

It has been proven that disabilities can be transformed into abilities when handicapped people have the opportunity to work with plants. Opening the doors for the use of these skills in employment and recreation is the objective of an international organization, the National Council for Therapy and Rehabilitation Through Horticulture, founded in 1973. The Council, with headquarters at the National Center for Horticulture, Mount Vernon, Virginia 22121, promotes and encourages the development of horticulture and related activities as a therapeutic and rehabilitation medium. It coordinates many professional, educational, therapeutic, and rehabilitative organizations that are striving to use horticulture in the course of human development.

Although the NCTRH has hundreds of success stories on file, these five give an idea of the wide applications of horticultural therapy:

1. A young woman who is responsible for the mounting, labeling, and storing of rare plant specimens at the National

Arboretum in Washington, D.C., is a graduate of the Melwood Horticultural Training Center for the Retarded.

2. In the state institution for the emotionally disturbed in Milledgeville, Georgia, where horticulture has been used to re-motivate the severely regressed, the patients respond remark-ably. One group of ten women had been given up as hopeless. Soon after an introduction to plant therapy they walked almost half a mile to the greenhouse and everyone talked sensibly. Eight of the women went home within two months; the other two did not have a home to go to.

3. A former warden at Statesville Penitentiary in Illinois has reported that he has been able to rehabilitate some of the tough-est psychological criminals only by means of horticultural therapy.

4. A nurseryman-florist who became blind has had to make many adaptations in his greenhouse procedures, but this has not affected the quality of the plants he grows. Today he en-courages other blind people, especially children, to visit his suc-cessful business so he can share the satisfaction he gains from caring for nature's gifts.

5. Over 75 percent of the graduates of the nation's institu-tions for horticultural therapy and rehabilitation have gone into jobs related to their training or have found their job training has made employment more accessible to them. One seventy-year-old graduate built a greenhouse in her back yard to sell bedding plants and dish gardens as an income supplement to social security; two mildly retarded brothers work in commer-cial greenhouses in their home town; one visually handicapped person with poor coordination opened a greenhouse to earn a living; another graduate is working at a greenhouse to help pay college expenses; others are in buildings and grounds mainte-nance, nurseries, parks—wherever the skills of horticulture pro-vide fulfilling employment.

Because plant therapy is being used successfully in various situations, each is considered separately in this chapter. The programs I have chosen to include represent only a sampling of the remarkable work being done today by concerned, caring individuals and organizations in all parts of the country, as well as Canada and England.

The Physically Handicapped

Dr. Howard A. Rusk, director of the Institute of Rehabilitation Medicine, New York University Medical Center, in his foreword to *Horticulture As a Therapeutic Aid,* by Howard D. Brooks and Charles J. Oppenheim, writes:

The Therapeutic Greenhouse at the Institute was born at a party in 1959 where I met Mrs. Ira Haupt, who was then the dynamic, imaginative editor of *Seventeen* magazine. She told me that she had a foundation and helped many causes, but this gave her no satisfaction or sense of accomplishment. She said, "If you know of a project in which I can get really interested and give of myself as well as my substance, let me know." I knew that she was tremendously interested in flowers and growing things and understood the therapy that comes with digging in the ground and planting seeds that create beauty. I thought long and hard about this challenge during dinner, and at coffee I told her I felt I had the answer. The Institute had just been built and we were already crowded with severely disabled and distressed human beings. I told her that I felt the creation of a therapeutic greenhouse would be' incalculable inspiration to those courageous people who were actually fighting for their lives. To work in it would be to help them live with dignity and independence. She liked the idea and the Therapeutic Greenhouse was born. It included a beautiful reflection pool that could be used by the children for wading; wide aisles so that wheelchairs could go between benches; planters with bright flowers, and also birds and fish. There was a special room where the patients could come and work, water and cultivate their own plants, and thus create their own beauty. This new, unique place of healing was dedicated in May of 1959. Hundreds of patients through the years have not only found joy and solace in the program but many have gone on to follow careers in horticulture or as florists. Distressed families have found peace in the atmosphere.

Typical of Institute patients' responses are these two letters received by Howard D. Brooks, horticulturist at the Institute. The first read, in part: "I have been home two weeks and I seem to have made the transition with no difficulty. 'My garden' which you so generously provided is a source of fun and satisfaction. Every afternoon I spend some time with it." The writer was a hemiplegic. The second letter reminded Mr. Brooks that "I was a stroke patient and you helped me make a terrarium . . . I was quite proud of it since it was the first and only thing I have done with the use of one arm only. By the way, I would like to try one more. Do you know of a seed or plant supplier who has a catalog I can write for?"

As explained in *Horticulture As a Therapeutic Aid*, the Horticultural Therapy program at the Institute is one aspect of the total rehabilitation of the patient.

Activities are based on the goals established for the individual by an occupational or physical therapist. The program also may provide assessment of vocational potential and performance evaluation reports. Patients may work alone or in small groups, once a week or more often—depending upon assignment, degree of interest, physical or mental limitations, age and need for supervision. For some, the program is an opportunity to resume a hobby, thereby re-establishing a link with life outside the hospital. For others, it may be a new and exciting experience. Where feasible, programs are planned to be carried on at home after the patient's discharge. In very basic terms, the horticultural practices used in the greenhouse are related to the patient's own personal life and physical restrictions. The simplest instruments are used—those readily available in the home.

In planning the activities, emphasis is placed on reinforcing physical gains being made in the other therapy areas. Equally important, however, are the intellectual, social and psychological benefits. Conferences are held with the occupational therapist or therapists associated in other areas of treatment. Often, the doctor in charge of the patient is consulted to determine the specific goals to be established. Then, if possible, a normal horticultural routine is adapted to fit the actual needs of the patient. Among other physical advantages, this helps in developing hand function, such as improving grasp, pinch and/or dexterity.

Other therapeutic uses of horticulture at the Institute check counting and numbers sense, color sense, coordination, alignment and space concepts.

There are many psychological aspects to and benefits from horticultural therapy as practiced at the Institute. Some patients are difficult to reach and motivate. Working with plants may provide an impetus and initiate a response. Something as simple as the growth of roots on a cutting suspended in a glass of water, or a bud preparing to open, may provide the key. One of the great advantages of gardening is that it is not a static activity. There is always something happening—a new sprout, shoot or leaf is forming, a flower is opening or fading and has to be removed. Then the cycle begins all over again. Most important, especially for patients who are totally dependent on others for assistance in even the smallest tasks, is a living thing depending on *them* for care and sustenance. This gives the patient the will to go on and an interest in the future. A plant needs to be watered, transplanted, given more or less light, cultivated, fed, and groomed. (These are basic routines of life that the patients themselves understand.) It also gives them the knowledge of success or failure based on their ability to meet the needs of the plant in their care. All this helps them make a greater effort on their own behalf, something to which they can relate in a very personal way.

All age groups benefit from working with growing plants. The youngest child, on the threshold of so many new experiences, is fascinated by the diversity of seed shapes, colors and textures—as he is with the living plant material itself. For many children this is a whole new world filled with beauty and pleasure.

Adults, at first, have to overcome the trauma of whatever misfortune has befallen them. Then, they welcome horticultural therapy as either an escape from the present, or a return to the security of prior familiarity. Those who have gardened before may welcome it as an opportunity to lose themselves and awareness of their handicaps for a brief time. This, of course, will depend upon the degree of physical damage. Some may reject it if their ability to do the vigorous tasks associated with outdoor gardening has been compromised. If they have had indoor gardening experience, acceptance will be more likely because gross activity demands will be fewer. If they are familiar with growing plants under artificial lights and micro-climate conditions, acceptance will be even quicker.

The most difficult group will be the males from early teens to middle twenties. In most instances, they will reject this form of therapy, particularly if they are unfamiliar with gardening. This is true, principally, of the paraplegic whose masculinity is threatened, he feels, by the sudden reversal of roles in which he finds himself—dependent, to an agonizing degree, upon others. He is seldom capable of participating in what, to him, seems a feminine activity.

The relation between a patient and the plant he has brought into being by sowing seeds, propagating and finally potting is truly meaningful. Curiosity, concern and hope itself will be aroused in the person who has accepted the responsibility for giving a plant the essential of life. This can be a rewarding and health-giving experience.

With the awakening of a greater interest in the relation of

man to his environment, plants provide a vital key to understanding biology—the science of life. Gardening offers an opportunity to become involved in this biological world on whatever level desired. Working with the soil, and following the cycles of the plant world upon which man is dependent, brings an involvement and an awareness of everything around us. With this comes appreciation and reaction to the impact we make upon our environment whether it be good or bad.

Alice W. Burlingame, who is renowned for her work as a horticultural therapist and is the author of *Hoe for Health,* knows that plant therapy can be adapted to all diagnoses and all ages. Among her many interesting projects for both hospital and home patients is her plan to "substitute a hoe for a cane." She encourages the cane user working in a garden to "stand with his feet 15 inches apart and to use a tool with a long handle, always knowing he can lean on the handle for support if necessary. A cane can be a buddy, providing assurance and allowing new levels of performance, or it can become a crutch and curb the goals of rehabilitation." She also knows that outdoor gardening is a creation with many rewards: exercise, relaxation, achievement, anticipation, creativity, beautification and, best of all, fun.

Horticultural therapy programs in veterans' facilities, hospitals and nursing homes, prisons, schools of special education, and for homebound patients—all have need for volunteers from the community. Ms. Burlingame's *Hoe for Health* makes these suggestions for establishing such a program:

> To be successful, every program should have a sponsor. An interested volunteer should go to his church, P-TA, garden club or civic organization and interest the total membership in sponsoring a horticultural therapy program. This is important in order to assure continuity of contact with patients. A program

cannot be dependent upon the attendance of one person. Ill people should not be disappointed. It is logical to expect that the active team of workers may be small; but, from time to time, members from the total membership of the sponsoring organization will want to assist with securing needed supplies.

Sponsors for such a recognized therapy will give prestige to the program and to the institution receiving the service. Not everyone can work easily with patients, but the non-contact workers often are important members of the team as they gather flowers, seeds, cuttings, pressed ribbons and sundry accessories to add zest to a presentation. Light refreshments are often welcome after a period of work; here again is a place for workers behind the scenes.

Who should be on the volunteer team for therapeutic gardening? The volunteer should work easily with others. The most important characteristic that this person should have is the ability to allow some of his "goodness" to rub off on the patient. The patient will benefit from cheerfulness, smiles, an inspirational character and the desire to assist him reach new levels of motivations.

The second attribute is a knowledge of flowers and plants. Just stop and think for a minute. When you are ill you aren't interested in anything complicated. So it is with our programs. They must be on an elementary level with variations to hold the interest of the patient.

Where shall we present this program? The first consideration of a locale is that the volunteers do not have to travel very far "to work," so that a good attendance is assured. This program has been successful in every type of hospital, in schools for the handicapped, for homebound children and adults, as well as in prison.

How do we make our contact? In hospitals we like to work through the occupational therapy department or the hospital school program. This provides constant professional guidance to assure success. The special education department of the schools will welcome a program. The warden of a prison will readily recognize all facets of benefits as the community is brought to his wards. For the homebound, you work through the family with the knowledge of the attending physician.

We now have eager workers with a sponsoring group. We know where we want to work. How do we raise the curtain on therapy through horticulture? Plan on a work session of three hours every two or three months. For one-third of the period have a guest speaker to orient the volunteer on subjects such as these: The Ethics in Our Hospital; The Psychology of Selling Your Ideas to Others; The Current Story of Epilepsy; How Much Work Can Heart Cases Do?; All About House Plants; Working with Dried Materials; Holiday Ideas from Plant Materials; How to Make a Terrarium. You can comb your community for good speakers, and your volunteers will delight in their new education.

The last two hours of the volunteer meeting should be used to plan work periods for patients up to the next meeting. Plan the nature of the program and list the materials needed. It is very stimulating to have rotating chairmen of the month. In this way, you will develop leadership that will be invaluable to the general chairman. The total program will have more sparkle. The other volunteers will, of course, assist the chairman of the day.

One program might be the making of corsages and flower arrangements. Other possible programs are the sowing of seeds in pots and open gardens, the propagation of cuttings, an outdoor garden, the care of house plants, bulb forcing, a terrarium, a bottle garden, visits to local gardens and flower shows, or work in a greenhouse. Homebound patients, especially those who have had a cerebral accident (stroke), benefit from working in their home gardens. Here the volunteer's task is to quicken the patient's interest with plants new in his experience. Motivation of these patients is brought to a new level by the performance of many routine gardening tasks with the volunteer as a companion gardener.

Eleanore McCurry, an occupational therapist at Clinton Valley Center, in Pontiac, Michigan, says that state hospitals seem always to suffer from limited budgets and each of their plant programs has been financed almost entirely by the garden club which sponsors it. Flowers are usually contributed by funeral homes or florists—the latter donating flowers that have been cut for several days and haven't been sold. A national seed company interested in the therapeutic results of gardening donates vegetable seeds. Other supplies are often furnished by the garden clubs themselves, as they may generously appropriate a certain amount of their budget to support horticultural therapy.

The Mentally Retarded

Earl Copus, Jr., director of Melwood Training Center for the Retarded, Upper Marlboro, Maryland, writing in *Landscape for Living* (published by the United States Department of Agriculture in 1972), tells of a young man who greeted a newcomer to the center with the words, "I used to be retarded." The center is devoted exclusively to mentally retarded boys and girls, and this greeting shows the transformation in attitude that takes place within a few weeks after the young people start their training.

The first step in the transformation takes place when the young person checks in. A young man who arrives at the Center as "little Jimmie," even though he may be 17 or 18 years old, is introduced to the other trainees as Jim. He is told he will be treated as a man, and that he will be expected to act like one. As often happens when a person knows he is expected to behave a certain way, Jim accepts his changed status and responds like a young man.

At the Melwood Horticultural Training Center, new ground

is being broken in the lives of the mentally retarded—in the greenhouses, potting sheds and classrooms—to provide career opportunities that most of the handicapped, and their families, had never dreamed possible.

Melwood was established in 1963 by a group of parents who believed that a plant-growing environment would be an ideal one in which to develop job responsibility, basic work skills, and employability in mentally limited young people. The convictions of these parents were strong; some were professional horticulturists as well as the parents of mentally retarded children.

By late 1971, some 60 trainees were enrolled, 40 boys and 20 girls, in the regular daytime program. Their I.Q.'s vary from a low of 40 to a high of 100, with an average of 60-70.

The center now earns 40 percent of its total income. It is otherwise supported by funds from the State, county, private organizations and dedicated citizens.

The newer boys are kept close to the center until they get to know a little about working with the plants and learn some self-sufficiency. They are always keen, though, to go out on the truck with the experienced boys to work in the fields.

Young women in vocational training participate in a program emphasizing greenhouse and floral design skills, both at the center and in the community. The center's own floral shop provides valuable contacts with customers as well as vocational experience.

The work experience program is designed for the person who requires an extensive personal and vocational adjustment. It is like the vocational program except that it is much more individualized.

Approximately 20 to 30 trainees a year attain community employment. The job responsibility and work habits they acquire also qualify them for employment in other kinds of jobs—like stockroom helper, labor helper, and clerical aide.

Melwood is proof that a horticultural environment opens training and career opportunities for the mentally limited. It has been so successful that it has attracted national attention, and Melwood's format is being copied in other communities.

Bob Detwiler has worked with young adult retarded males for a number of years in New Mexico. He believes that

> Every human being has a God-given intelligence which is innate. This intelligence can only be expressed by means of a well-developed nervous system. Parts of the expression of this intelligence (such as speech, reading, writing or numerical abilities) may be blocked due to damage to the nervous system. When this happens, we must first try to restore the nervous system through physical training and rehabilitation. At the same time, and especially if the damage is severe, we should find alternate ways in which the intelligence can be expressed. Some of these alternate means are: work activities, play, arts and crafts, and agriculture. There is a kind of natural feedback mechanism involved in working with plants: by their very flourishing, our plants show us the right way to work with them. Thus they validate our innate intelligence.

The Visually Handicapped

Mr. Copus says that the use of horticulture as training, career opportunity, and therapy for the handicapped is on the increase. A program called Greenhouse and Nursery Training for the Blind was set up in 1955 and sponsored jointly by the Office of Rehabilitation, the U.S. Department of Health, Education and Welfare, and the Department of Education at the Georgia Academy for the Blind at Macon, Georgia. "It was their purpose" Copus writes, "to invent special techniques and provide special training to enable sight-handicapped persons to achieve the same horticultural objectives as persons with unimpaired sight. The amazing thing about this project is that those sight-handicapped persons learned, physically and psychologically, to become useful employees for many of the usual tasks in greenhouses and nurseries. Thus, working with plants as therapy in some instances leads to employment itself."

A way for the visually handicapped to enjoy nature is to visit what is commonly called a Braille Trail, where all labels are in Braille and the unsighted person can touch ferns, smell the balsam aroma, and listen to the sounds of stream, birds, small animals, and the wind in the trees. Some work has been done with the very young visually handicapped who were helped to plant pumpkin and giant sunflower seeds. They realized their achievement when they felt the pumpkins and sunflowers—and became more interested in plants.

The Emotionally Disturbed

The Menninger Clinic is a private psychiatric hospital in Topeka, Kansas, where the use of horticulture as a therapy has a long history. Dr. C. F. Menninger was a keen horticulturist, led nature walks on the hospital grounds, and instilled the love of nature in staff as well as patients. Two of his sons, Dr. Karl and Dr. Will Menninger, followed in his footsteps at the hospital and also became practicing horticulturists.

With this background it is natural for the Menninger hospital to use varying forms of horticulture in patient treatment. Gardening as a therapeutic tool began after World War II, and greenhouse activity was begun there by Rhea McCandliss in the late 1950s.

Patients meet daily for two hours in the large greenhouse or work in the outside flower beds. Andrew Barber, who is in charge of greenhouse activity, says, "We are using education, work, group interaction, relationships with a therapist, delayed gratification, and most importantly the development of responsibility as therapeutic tools." In his capacity as director of the Horticultural Therapy Training Program in cooperation with Kansas State University, he works to "enhance the student's academic horticultural and psychological training with practical job experience in a psychiatric hospital."

Dr. John A. Talbott, director of Comprehensive Clinical Services at the Payne Whitney Clinic of New York Hospital, in his work with chronically ill mental patients, has studied the effect of patients' observing flowering plants during mealtimes. He found that patients spent more time at the table, ate better, had more eye contact with each other, and talked to each other more often. Moreover, when the staff became involved with caring for the flowering plants, their morale improved.

It is known that the emotionally disturbed often suffer from loneliness, anxiety, boredom, and a feeling of not being needed. Working with living plant material and being stimulated by the color and beauty of plants and flowers leads to the realization that plants "need us," as well as filling a pocket of time in a creative, satisfying way that increases feelings of personal importance and worth. When topped off with praise from a staff member, volunteer, or visitor, self-security begins to renew itself.

Drug Abusers

Although horticultural therapy has only recently been added to a few rehabilitation programs for drug abusers, it is already established that plants are nonthreatening to most of them. This is important because drug patients usually have problems relating to other people and suffer from low self-esteem. Some who have felt they were not intelligent have learned through step-by-step plant therapy that they are intelligent and that they can learn. As more and more trained horticultural therapists become available, both professional and volunteer, plants will play an increasing role in helping drug addicts reconstruct their lives.

Potential High School Dropouts

The New York Botanical Garden offered a trainee-gardener program, funded by Mrs. Arthur Hays Sulzberger, for potential high-school dropouts. The course combined an abbreviated scholastic program with actual gardening field work and instruction at the Botanical Garden. Students received a small monthly income. Out of a pilot group of sixty boys only one failed to complete the high-school course. In addition to his regular diploma, each boy received a certificate in gardening from the Botanical Garden. This project was so successful that it was taken over by New York City and paid for, for a time, by the Human Resources Administration. The program motivated the boys to remain in school and a large number of them continued in the field of horticulture after graduation.

Training in Horticultural Therapy

Training in horticultural therapy is offered to volunteers who work with homebound patients and to the personnel of social agencies by the Horticultural Society of New York. Volunteers take a twelve-session training course, after which each works with one or two homebound clients on a weekly basis. Follow-up conferences are held periodically with the director. Social agency personnel come from those working with senior citizens, from nursing homes, from recreation and social service departments of hospitals. Veterans' facilities and any social agency or health organization interested in starting a program of horticultural therapy are encouraged to send staff members for training.

Of the twelve colleges and universities listed below, six offer courses but no degree and six offer a degree in horticultural therapy.

Colleges That Offer a Degree in Horticultural Therapy

CLEMSON UNIVERSITY
Department of Horticulture
Clemson, South Carolina 29631
Attention: Dr. T. L. Senn

UNIVERSITY OF FLORIDA
Department of Horticulture
113 Rolfs Hall
Gainesville, Florida 32611
Attention: Dr. G. Shannon Smith

KANSAS STATE UNIVERSITY
Department of Horticulture
Manhattan, Kansas 66504
Attention: Dr. Ronald Campbell

MICHIGAN STATE UNIVERSITY
Department of Horticulture
East Lansing, Michigan 48824
Attention: Dr. J. Lee Taylor

UNIVERSITY OF RHODE ISLAND
Department of Plant and Soil Science
Kingston, Rhode Island 02881
Attention: Walter Larmie

TEXAS TECH UNIVERSITY
Department of Park Administration and Horticulture
Lubbock, Texas 79409
Attention: Dr. George Tereshkovich

Colleges That Offer Horticultural Therapy but No Degree

COLORADO STATE
Department of Horticulture
Fort Collins, Colorado 80521

COLORADO WOMEN'S COLLEGE
1700 Pontiac Street
Denver, Colorado 80220
Attention: Professor Exie White

UNIVERSITY OF GEORGIA
Department of Horticulture
Plant Science Building
Athens, Georgia 30601
Attention: Nicholas Natarella

IOWA LAKES COMMUNITY COLLEGE
Agricultural Education
3200 College Drive
Emmettsburg, Iowa 50536

UNIVERSITY OF MARYLAND
Department of Horticulture
College Park, Maryland 20742
Attention: Dr. Conrad B. Link

PENNSYLVANIA STATE UNIVERSITY
Department of Horticulture
103 Tyson Boulevard
University Park, Pennsylvania 19802
Attention: Dr. R. Stinson

The adaptability and success of horticultural therapy is based on the fact that man and plants exist side by side in nature. Thus contact with orderly cycles of nature has a curative effect on the development of the individual intellectually, emotionally, socially, and physically. Through horticultural therapy patients learn to appreciate natural surroundings. Powers of observation are sharpened. People respond to watching things grow and feel a sense of responsibility to a plant that depends on them. They learn at first hand the central proposition of this book, that people need plants and plants need people.

10 ❧ Nature Without a Garden

❧ There are times when it may be inconvenient or impossible to have a garden of your own, either indoors or outdoors. Ironically, this may occur when you most need contact with nature, perhaps while away from home on business for a long time or living briefly in a strange city.

Fortunately, you don't have to have a garden or be a gardener in order to appreciate public displays of flowers and plants. Take a walk and see what you can find to give your spirits a lift. Feast your eyes on the flowers and plants displayed in the lighted window of a flower shop on a cold night. If street litter bothers you, try looking up at the trees—which do grow along some streets of every city, even mine, contrary to what some people may say. Subway flower stalls are not to be overlooked either as a source of contact with nature. I suppose I am a plant voyeur, but I get tremendous pleasure just walking at night along the streets of New York or any other city and looking up at lighted apartments and offices to find windows filled with plants.

In recent years there has been a decided increase in the use of living plants in the lobbies of commercial buildings. That of the Ford Foundation on East Forty-second Street in New York is perhaps the most remarkable, but hardly a block in the city is without some encouraging display of plants in a lobby or storefront. This is true of cities and towns all over the country. Whenever I see a particularly beautiful planting I try to note the name and address and send a note of appreciation; by the same token, when I see a major planting of plastic plants and flowers, obviously installed at considerable expense, I write a letter to the president of the firm suggesting how much more effective live plants would be.

The public botanical gardens and arboreta (collections of woody plant materials, primarily trees and shrubs) of this country—and the world—offer endless opportunities for brief but beneficial encounters with plants. Lately I have noticed a tremendous increase in the number of visitors at such places as Longwood Gardens, Kennett Square, Pennsylvania; the Brooklyn Botanic Garden, in New York City; and the Golden Gate Park Conservatory, in San Francisco. Lest you think I indulge my passion for plants by flying around to visit places like these, this is not the case. When I travel it is usually on business. Visiting the local public gardens helps keep me from being homesick, and observing how the professionals cultivate and display plants gives me ideas that I put into practice myself or report in my writings. When possible, I like to time my visits on a weekday, so that the crowds will be smaller and the gardeners responsible for growing the plants are more likely to be around in case I want to ask questions.

Any time you feel the need for exposure to flowers and plants, check the local newspaper for announcements of flower shows. The major spring flower shows in such cities as Boston, Philadelphia, and Chicago offer inspiration to the gardener and nongardener alike. But these are only a small percentage of the total. Most of the plant societies listed in Chapter 8 stage local, regional, and national exhibits on a regular basis, not to mention the nearly countless flower shows sponsored by local garden clubs. Spring, summer, and early autumn are the most popular times, but in the period between Thanksgiving and Christmas there are exhibits showing the use of fresh and dried plant materials in holiday decorations, and many of the plant societies have local shows in midwinter.

An active interest in plants not only makes routine travels more interesting; it can also increase the pleasure of traveling for pleasure. Plants, flowers, and gardens offer beautiful and challenging subjects for photography. My preference is to travel with two cameras, one for black-and-white, one for color transparencies. Back at home I have the photographs to recall my travels, and sometimes I refer to them when I feel like dabbling with water colors or acrylic paints, or I may use one as the basis for a needlepoint design. On one visit to the Keukenhof Gardens, in Holland, I spent several days photographing tulips, daffodils, hyacinths, and other bulb flowers, many of them as reflections in water. After the trip I edited these, mixing the reflections with dramatic closeups and long shots of the bulb gardens, until one slide tray was filled. These were projected on a wall of my living room during a candlelighted cocktail party, with the projector set to change the picture automatically every thirty seconds. It proved a highly successful diversion for the guests and allowed me to share my trip without feeling that my audience was captive.

Whether or not you have a garden, flower arranging offers another opportunity for involvement with nature. It can be as simple or complicated, as inexpensive or costly as you like.

When I am traveling, a single stem of freesias or a bunch of daffodils purchased from a neighborhood florist is all I need to make what I consider a successful flower arrangement. At home I gladly practice petty economies to save enough money to buy a few fresh-cut flowers. My preference is to select what is in season; that gives you the most for the money and is a pleasant reminder of the changing seasons.

One way I enjoy arranging flowers at home is to place each stem in a separate small container of water. These miniatures can be arranged in an infinite number of ways to create the desired effect for a dinner-table centerpiece, a cocktail table, a night stand in the bedroom, or the bathroom counter. Having each stem in a separate container gives complete freedom to arrange and rearrange, to throw out wilted flowers without disturbing those still fresh.

If you want to make an arrangement of flowers in one container, florists' foam makes it easy to achieve whatever effect you want, at the same time securely anchoring and holding the blooms exactly where you think they look the most beautiful. If the bouquet contains several different colors as well as different kinds of flowers, one way to create a beautiful arrangement is to keep flowers of a kind and color massed more or less together, as if you had walked through a garden with a pail of water and a pair of shears, first cutting yellow roses from one bush and putting them together in the pail, then some white iris from a clump, and Shasta daisies or feverfew from yet another. If you reconstruct in an arrangement the appearance these flowers had when just picked and grouped by kind in a pail, you will be amazed at how beautiful they will look in your arrangement.

Another way to create a bouquet is to select as many different kinds of flowers as possible within the same color range—for example, from palest pink to the dark, almost black red of some roses. Cut the stems at varying lengths, so that each flower stands out as if inviting you to touch or smell it.

I always enjoy seeing a bunch of one kind of flower, all of the same color, displayed in a vase or other container. In a silver cylinder ten inches tall and two inches in diameter I often place ten stems of blue Dutch iris. In a crystal bowl three inches deep I sometimes put a needle flower holder in the bottom, add a bunch of daffodils, then hide the mechanics by filling the bowl with clean pebbles or little seashells, after which I add water until it is not quite visible on the surface. One stem of a spider chrysanthemum can be elegant indeed in a beautiful vase; a few short-stemmed carnations bunched together make a nosegay for a low container.

It is fun to arrange fresh flowers with vegetables and fruit. My aim when I do this is to enjoy the edibles perhaps for only an evening as the centerpiece for a dinner party. After my guests leave I rinse the vegetables and fruit in water, dry them, and store them in the refrigerator. Whatever flowers I may have used I then fashion into some other kind of arrangement. Some of my favorite vegetables and fruits for this decorative use include asparagus spears, broccoli and cauliflower (both of which may be broken or cut apart if the individual head is too large), eggplant, yellow summer squash, apples, bananas, lemons and limes. A typical arrangement is to use a shallow market basket, perhaps twelve by twenty-four inches by five inches deep. I use a bread pan to hold a block of water-soaked florists' foam and place this inside the basket. Then I arrange the flowers in this, and work the fruits and vegetables all around so that the effect is that of just-picked harvest from the garden.

Flower arranging is something that can be immensely rewarding and enjoyable for men and women, children and adults. Some people have the idea that arranging flowers is the sole domain of women and professional floral designers, but the horticultural therapist Rhea McCandliss writes of her experiences at the Menninger Clinic, "Because there is a good deal of heavy work connected with the greenhouse, I have sometimes worried because we kept the men patients so busy mixing soil and wheeling sand that they didn't get to learn enough about the planting and care of plants, or to do the fun things. So when a man watching a woman arrange flowers said, 'I bet I could do that,' I never said that is for women to do, but rather, 'Some of the best florist designers are men. Go ahead and try it.' And sometimes they did a better job than the women patients."

The art of flower arranging goes far beyond the ideas I have suggested. The Japanese art of flower arranging, known as ikebana, is widely practiced today in this country; there is a national organization (the address is listed in Chapter 8), and it has many local branches where you can learn the art and make new friends at the same time.

Flower arranging can be a consuming interest for the person who is wholly or partly immobilized by a serious illness. I first became aware of this when it was my good fortune to become friends with Lillian Lewis Bodine, who suffered from crippling arthritis and was confined to a wheelchair. She had boundless enthusiasm for life in general, and spent most of her time creating exquisite flower arrangements for her home and presenting lecture-demonstrations for the inspiration and education of thousands of people. Her audiences not only admired her artistry but found it all the more meaningful because of her limited circumstances.

Some would-be gardeners are frustrated because they have no plot of ground to call their own, to plan, dig, sow seeds, and nurture. If this is your dilemma, involvement in a community gardening project may be the answer. All across the country community gardens have been springing up in recent years. Vacant lots are being cleaned up and reclaimed as places where residents from the surrounding neighborhood can plant vegetables, herbs, and flowers. Companies in executive or industrial parks are plowing up a few acres of grass and staking out plots in which individual employees can grow vegetables and flowers. If you would like to become involved in a community gardening project, get in touch with any local garden club or horticultural society, your county agriculture extension agent (who represents the United States Department of Agriculture), or propose such a project to the management of your company.

Another way to find yourself a place to garden is to become a volunteer gardener for a botanical garden. Most of these desperately need more help than they can afford to pay. Volunteers play an important role at the Missouri Botanical Garden, in St. Louis, and in the future we can expect an increasing number of public gardens to work out the necessary details in order to take advantage of willing helpers, often retired people, who are not only experienced, but may have a dedication that exceeds that of the paid nine-to-fivers.

Community beautification offers an unlimited opportunity to garden when you have no garden. The Magnolia Tree Earth Center of Bedford-Stuyvesant, in Brooklyn, New York, is an outstanding example. It is the result of efforts by Mrs. Hattie Carthan and other community volunteers who managed to save a glorious ninety-year-old magnolia tree and the brownstones adjacent to it. Since that time more than fifteen hundred trees have been planted in the Bedford-Stuyvesant area, with the New York City Parks Department joining in a tree-matching program. Youngsters from nine to fifteen have joined the Tree Corps and are responsible for maintaining the trees. All this came about after six years of bureaucratic struggle, during which the group dealt with city officials, architects, administrators, urban planners, educators, and community people to formulate working plans for the center, and obtained from the Model Cities Administration money to build a forty-foot wall to protect the magnolia tree.

The residents of a depressed area in Portland, Oregon, began their "Green Fingers" project after an imaginative member of the Oregon Federation of Garden Clubs got the idea that her organization might sponsor a vegetable gardening project; the aid of a black real-estate broker was enlisted and the program was on its way. The State Highway Commission lent some land; fertilizer manufacturers, pesticide formulators, and civic clubs donated their goods and time; equipment was lent or donated; and the entire community, from tots to retired people, got busy. Fear of vandalism was short-lived, owing to the number of people involved in making the project a success. The spirit in the community generated both volunteer watches and a feeling of respect for the gardens, which by this time had given a new life and hope to the community.

Inner-city gardeners can discover in their work new, life-enhancing values. Growing plants and vegetables suggests the possibility of, and patterns for, beauty and order in other parts of one's life.

11 🌿 Plants for Confidence

🌿 One reason plants are therapeutic is that caring for their needs helps us become less self-involved. Another is that the rewards are tangible—a new leaf, a fragrant flower, an off-spring. When you adopt a plant as your responsibility and it responds well to you, it increases your confidence not only as a gardener but as a person. That's why I want to list in this chapter the best confidence builders I know.

If you've never before accepted the sole responsibility for a living plant, give yourself a break. Start with one, two, maybe three. Whether or not you talk to your plants, it takes time to get acquainted with the needs of each different one. Having to meet the differing needs of too many plants all at once can cause needless anxiety.

There are two basic approaches to selecting plants. One is to choose what appeals to you and worry later about whether or not you can provide the environment it needs. If you're lucky, there'll be no worries later, but if you have adopted the most beautiful plant you could find and it begins to die, your psyche will suffer.

◄ The other approach, which I consider far safer if you want plants to be therapeutic and not traumatic, is to evaluate thoughtfully the environment in which you want to grow one or more plants. Whether it is to be indoors or outdoors, your considerations will be similar, but for the sake of simplicity let's talk about the interior environment. You'll need answers to these questions:

How much direct sunlight reaches the sill, table top, floor, or other space to be occupied by the plant?

Is there no direct sun? If not, is the natural light bright enough to read or do needlepoint? If not, consider supplementary artificial light.

What temperature range will the plant experience? If you want to be sure, place a thermometer in the part of the room where you want to grow plants. Check and write down temperature readings at various times of the day and night. Knowing for sure can make a big difference to the plant you befriend.

How much humidity is in the air? Most houses and apartments have an atmosphere in winter that is too dry for plant comfort, not to mention that of people and fine wood furnishings. A hygrometer is the instrument used to measure relative humidity; one may be purchased from the local hardware store, by mail from major catalogs, or from some specialists in supplies for the indoor gardener. The humidity in my apartment ranges between 30 and 45 percent in winter. To maintain this in coldest weather, when maximum heat is required, I use a small electric cool-vapor humidifier in each room.

When you have answers to all these questions, you're ready to shop for plants and see what you like. (If you intend to shop by mail, consult the list of sources at the end of the chapter.) At this point, having the help of someone who is a true plant person is essential. But don't misunderstand, paying a high price won't necessarily buy the best plant or the best advice. If you find yourself baffled and with no reliable help in sight, write down the names of the plants you like best and look up their needs in a book.

Full-disclosure labeling of plants is now under consideration by the Federal Trade Commission, but some sold today are improperly labeled or have no labels at all. If a plant you like is not labeled and no one can tell you the name, you (and it) might be better off if you first tried to find its picture in an illustrated and comprehensive reference book such as Alfred Byrd Graf's *Exotica*. If no identity can be established, buy the plant only if you're truly committed to discovering its needs. In this kind of situation I would give a plant with thin, delicate leaves bright light but little or no direct sun; a plant with thick, glossy, leathery, or succulent leaves direct sun for a few hours daily. And in all cases I would keep the soil nicely moist; never at either extreme of being so wet that water remains for days at a time in the saucer or so dry that the soil surface feels brick-hard or dusty. It would also be a good idea to position the plant so that no drafts of hot or cold air blow directly on it. If you begin with this middle-of-the-road approach, you and your plant will likely grow to understand each other.

All you have to do is succeed with one plant and you will have vaulted the green-thumb barrier. Forget past failures. Forget every plant except the one you are going to succeed with. The moment you realize that you and your plant have got it together you will never forget. Never.

Do you know why those of us who love gardening never stop growing and looking for new plants with which to make friends? Because every time a plant responds favorably to you, the miracle happens again. It's the same as eating good food when you're hungry, drinking good wine when you're thirsty, making love with the right person when you're feeling romantic.

If you are just getting started with plants, do some scouting around before you spend much money. Look in plant books, catalogs, and gardening magazines. See what is available that has special appeal to you. There are rare plants that may be far better for your circumstances than a house plant as common as pothos. And when an unusual plant begins to thrive for you, it will be a special ego builder.

As I suggested earlier, too much plant parenthood all at once can be bad. But if you find the idea of having only three plants in the beginning not very exciting, what if they were three unusual or spectacular plants—all as easy to grow as the most common ones you see all around? The twenty-five house plants described here were finally selected from a list of the hundred best diehards. They are included here as examples of some of the most beautiful and durable of all. Some are common, some are not. Sizes vary from tiny creeping baby's-tears to towering fig and palm trees. Every plant here has a disposition you can look forward to coming home to. But the more precisely you follow each plant's recipe for success in the beginning, the more likely you are to establish a lasting relationship.

If you build your plant collection slowly you'll be able to limit its content to the colors, shapes, forms, sizes, textures, and scents that fit well into your environment. And by now you must have decided along with me that creating a healthy environment for plants means you are creating a better environment for yourself.

If you give a plant your best attentions and it dies anyway, don't feel guilty. Try to analyze what went wrong. Even the world's superthumb gardeners have failures. I always hate to lose a plant, but sometimes I become a better gardener for it.

Plants to Build Your Confidence

AECHMEA

Pronunciation: ECK-me-uh
Common name: Bromeliad.
Uses: Desk top, wide sill, hanging basket, or pedestal.
Leaf color: Green, burgundy, silver.
Flowers: Pink, red, blue.

ENVIRONMENTAL NEEDS:

Light: Sunny east, south, or west window; tolerates bright light without direct sun indefinitely if mature to begin with; thrives in a fluorescent-light garden.

Temperature: 62-75 degrees F.

Humidity: Medium; tolerates less.

Mist frequently: Yes.

Soil mix: Cactus.

Soil moisture: Evenly moist to nearly dry; once a week fill cup formed by leaves with clean water, but pour out old water before adding fresh.

Propagation: By division, usually a few months after the plant has flowered.

Problems: None, unless roots stand in water for long periods of time.

Comments: Silver King aechmea is the most popular bromeliad sold by local florists and plant shops; other aechmeas, available from specialists, are also showy and easy to grow.

AESCHYNANTHUS

Pronunciation: esk-uh-NANTH-us
Common name: Lipstick vine
Uses: Hanging basket or pedestal.
Leaf color: Green; less common *A. marmoratus* has yellowish green and burgundy variegation.
Flowers: Red.

ENVIRONMENTAL NEEDS:
Light: Sunny east or west window; tolerates bright light without direct sun, but may not flower.
Temperature: 62-75 degrees F.
Humidity: Medium to high; tolerates less.
Mist frequently: Yes.
Soil mix: African violet or terrarium.
Soil moisture: Evenly moist; tolerates some dryness.
Propagation: Tip cuttings in any season.
Problems: Mealybugs may attack.
Comments: Lipstick vine is an unusually carefree basket or pedestal plant because the stems do not require pinching back; new growth, which sprouts from the base, keeps the plant looking full and compact.

AGLAONEMA

Pronunciation: ag-loh-NEE-muh

Common name: Chinese evergreen.

Uses: Desk top, sill or terrarium; a large aglaonema may be used for tree effect if displayed on a tall pedestal.

Leaf color: Green, silver, white, yellow, pink.

Flowers: White, similar to a calla-lily, followed by berries, at first green, then red.

ENVIRONMENTAL NEEDS:

Light: Bright, but little or no direct sun; young aglaonemas thrive in a fluorescent-light garden.

Temperature: 62-75 degrees F.

Humidity: Low to medium.

Mist frequently: Yes, if convenient.

Soil mix: All-purpose or African violet.

Soil moisture: Between nicely moist and wet.

Propagation: Tip cuttings in any season.

Problems: Trouble-free.

Comments: Aglaonema is one of the best of all foliage plants to cultivate in low-light areas; it will thrive in an office where the only light received is from ceiling fluorescents.

ALOE

Pronunciation: al-OH-ee

Common name: A. vera is sometimes called medicine or unguentine plant.

Uses: Desk top, sill, hanging basket, or pedestal.

Leaf color: Green, blue-green, sometimes variegated with white or silver.

Flowers: Rarely.

ENVIRONMENTAL NEEDS:

Light: Sunny east, south, or west window; small aloes will thrive in a fluorescent-light garden.

Temperature: 62-75 degrees F.

Humidity: Low.

Mist frequently: No.

Soil mix: Cactus.

Soil moisture: Between evenly moist and on the dry side.

Propagation: By division.

Problems: If chilled and wet at the same time, aloe roots may rot.

Comments: These succulent plants tolerate underwatering and neglect.

BEAUCARNEA

Pronunciation: boh-KARN-ee-uh
Common name: Ponytail; elephant's-foot.
Uses: Desk top or sill while young; older plants may be used as floor shrubs, for tree effect, in a hanging basket, or on a pedestal.
Leaf color: Green.
Flowers: No.

ENVIRONMENTAL NEEDS:
Light: Sunny east, south, or west window; tolerates bright light with little or no direct sun; young beaucarneas will thrive in a fluorescent-light garden.
Temperature: 62-75 degrees F.
Humidity: Low.
Mist frequently: No.
Soil mix: Cactus or all-purpose.
Soil moisture: Evenly moist to nearly dry.
Propagation: Occasionally by division.
Problems: If chilled and wet at the same time, the roots may rot.
Comments: Beaucarnea forms a large, bulblike growth that stores moisture; older specimens, especially, tolerate under-watering for long periods of time.

CHAMAEDOREA

Pronunciation: kam-uh-DOH-ree-uh.

Common name: Dwarf palm.

Uses: Desk top, sill, floor shrub, pedestal (if large, a pedestal-displayed chamaedorea may give the effect of a tree); fine for terrarium or bottle garden while young.

Leaf color: Green.

Flowers: Insignificant.

ENVIRONMENTAL NEEDS:

Light: Bright light or an hour or two of direct sun.

Temperature: 62-75 degrees F.

Humidity: Medium; tolerates less.

Mist frequently: Yes, if convenient.

Soil mix: All-purpose.

Soil moisture: Evenly moist.

Propagation: Division if multistemmed.

Problems: Red spider mites may attack if the atmosphere is hot, dry, and stale. Dry soil in combination with too much heat will cause tips of the fronds to die.

Comments: Chamaedorea elegans may eventually grow to six feet high; its variety *bella,* sometimes called *Neanthe bella,* grows only two or three feet high.

CHLOROPHYTUM

Pronunciation: kloh-roh-FYE-tum
Common name: Spider plant; airplane plant.
Uses: Desk top, sill, hanging basket or pedestal.
Leaf color: Green, or green and white.
Flowers: White, but insignificant.

ENVIRONMENTAL NEEDS:
Light: Bright light or near a sunny east, west, or south window; young plants of common spider plant and all sizes of miniature *C. bichettii* will thrive in a fluorescent-light garden.
Temperature: 62-75 degrees F.
Humidity: Medium; tolerates less.
Mist frequently: Yes, if convenient.
Soil mix: All-purpose.
Soil moisture: Evenly moist.
Propagation: Division or remove and plant the babies that form on the runners.
Problems: If the soil dries out severely, older leaves will die entirely and the tips of others will turn brown.
Comments: Opinions vary as to why common spider plants on occasion fail to send out runners with new plants; some authorities say the plant has to first fill the pot with roots, others say that too much artificial light at night delays or prevents runner growth.

COLEUS

Pronunciation: KOH-lee-us
Common name: Coleus.
Uses: Desk top, sill, hanging basket, pedestal.
Leaf color: Green, chartreuse, red, pink, burgundy.
Flowers: Blue, but insignificant; it is best to pinch off the buds before they develop.

ENVIRONMENTAL NEEDS:
Light: Sunny east, south, or west window; thrives in fluorescent-light garden.
Temperature: 62-75 degrees F.
Humidity: Medium; tolerates less.
Mist frequently: Yes, if convenient.
Soil mix: All-purpose, African violet, or terrarium.
Soil moisture: Evenly moist.
Propagation: Seeds or tip cuttings; easy.
Problems: Mealybugs seem to favor coleus over almost all other house plants; if you discover them on your coleus, probably the best thing to do is discard the entire plant and start over with a bug-free one. Coleus needs frequent pinching back to encourage compact, full growth.
Comments: One of the easiest of all house plants, but after a year or two the old stems become woody and tend to produce inferior growth; it's best to start new plants annually from tip cuttings or seeds.

DAVALLIA

Pronunciation: duh-VAL-lee-uh
Common name: Rabbit's-foot fern.
Uses: Desk top, sill, hanging basket, pedestal.
Leaf color: Green.
Flowers: No.

ENVIRONMENTAL NEEDS:

Light: Near a bright or sunny window, but sun shining directly on the leaves for more than an hour or two is not desirable.
Temperature: 62-75 degrees F.
Humidity: Medium.
Mist frequently: Yes, if convenient.
Soil mix: African violet or terrarium.
Soil moisture: Evenly moist.
Propagation: By rhizome cuttings.
Problems: Too much direct sun may cause new fronds to wither and die and older ones to develop brown leaflets; allowing the soil to dry out severely causes similar damage.
Comments: Although davallia is delicate in appearance, it is actually one of the easiest of all ferns to grow as a house plant.

DRACAENA

Pronunciation: druh-SEE-nuh
Common name: Corn plant, Madagascar dragon tree.
Uses: Desk top, sill, floor shrub, tree effect, or pedestal.
Leaf color: Green, or green with white, yellow, red, silver or pink.
Flowers: Small white and fragrant, but rarely.

ENVIRONMENTAL NEEDS:
Light: Near a bright or sunny window, but sun shining directly on the leaves for more than an hour or two is not required.
Temperature: 62-75 degrees F.
Humidity: Medium; tolerates less.
Mist frequently: Yes, if convenient.
Soil mix: All-purpose.
Soil moisture: Evenly moist to wet.
Propagation: Tip cuttings, division, or by air-layering.
Problems: Nearly trouble-free, but severely dry soil will cause the leaf tips to turn yellow or brown and die. *D. marginata* (Madagascar dragon tree) may drop quantities of the lower leaves if over- or underwatered.
Comments: *D. fragrans* (corn plant) and its variegated form, *massangeana,* are two of the best of all plants for low-light areas, along with *D. deremensis warneckei,* which has gray-green leaves distinctly striped with white.

EUCHARIS

Pronunciation: YEW-kuh-riss
Common name: Eucharist lily.
Uses: Desk top, wide sill, pedestal.
Leaf color: Dark green.
Flowers: White, occasionally; fragrant.

ENVIRONMENTAL NEEDS:
Light: Near a sunny east, south, or west window, but with little hot sun shining directly on the leaves.
Temperature: 62-75 degrees F.
Humidity: Medium; tolerates less.
Mist frequently: Yes, if convenient.
Soil mix: All-purpose.
Soil moisture: Evenly moist; after plant has filled the pot with roots and has many leaves, keeping it on the dry side and withholding fertilizer for two months, then resuming normal watering and feeding, should result in flower production.
Propagation: By division.
Problems: Virtually trouble-free.
Comments: Eucharis grows from a bulb; available from numerous mail-order firms (addresses at the end of this chapter). The leaves resemble those of spathiphyllum, but they have a more leathery quality and are less prone to brown tips. An outstanding house plant.

FICUS

Pronunciation: FYE-kuss

Common name: Weeping fig (*F. benjamina*), rubber tree (*F. elastica*), Indian laurel (*F. retusa nitida*), fiddleleaf fig (*F. lyrata*).

Uses: Floor shrub, tree, or pedestal plant.

Leaf color: Green.

Flowers: No.

ENVIRONMENTAL NEEDS:

Light: Near a sunny east, south, or west window. Insufficient light causes leaf drop, but ficus respond well to supplementary artificial light.

Temperature: 62-75 degrees F.

Humidity: Medium; tolerates less.

Mist frequently: Yes, if convenient.

Soil mix: All-purpose.

Soil moisture: Evenly moist.

Propagation: Stem cuttings or by air layering.

Problems: Red spider mites may attack if the air is hot, dry, and stale. If the soil dries out severely, heavy leaf drop will occur; if prolonged, entire branches may die. Too much hot sun shining directly on the leaves will cause yellow, brown or black burn spots.

Comments: Ficus are perhaps the best of all indoor plants where the effect of a leafy tree is desired.

HELXINE

Pronunciation: hel-ZYE-nee
Common name: Baby's-tears
Uses: Desk top, sill, hanging basket, pedestal or terrarium.
Leaf color: Green or golden green.
Flowers: No.

ENVIRONMENTAL NEEDS:
Light: Bright light or a few feet back from a sunny window; thrives in a fluorescent-light garden.
Temperature: 62-72 degrees F.
Humidity: Medium; tolerates less.
Mist frequently: Yes, if convenient.
Soil mix: African violet or terrarium.
Soil moisture: Evenly moist to wet.
Propagation: By division or tip cuttings.
Problems: Excessive heat and hot, dry air combination will quickly wither the delicate leaves and stems of baby's-tears.

HOWEIA

Pronunciation: HOW-ee-uh
Common name: Kentia palm
Uses: Floor shrub or tree effect.
Leaf color: Green.
Flowers: No.

ENVIRONMENTAL NEEDS:

Light: Near a sunny east, south, or west window; does fairly well in a bright exposure but without sun shining directly on the fronds.

Temperature: 62-75 degrees F.

Humidity: Medium; tolerates less.

Mist frequently: Yes, if convenient.

Soil mix: All-purpose.

Soil moisture: Evenly moist.

Propagation: By division, but difficult.

Problems: In hot, dry, stale air, red spider mite may attack. If the soil dries out severely, leaf tips will die.

Comments: This is one of the best of the large palms to cultivate indoors; it is coarser in appearance than the common areca, but *far* superior and worth the considerable price you will have to pay for a sizable, healthy specimen.

HOYA

Pronunciation: HOY-uh
Common name: Waxplant
Uses: Desk top, sill, hanging basket, pedestal, or terrarium.
Leaf color: Green, silver, white, rose-pink.
Flowers: White and pink; fragrant.

ENVIRONMENTAL NEEDS:

Light: Sunny east, south, or west window; adapts to bright light with little or no sun shining directly on the leaves; thrives in a fluorescent-light garden.
Temperature: 62-75 degrees F.
Humidity: Medium; tolerates less.
Mist frequently: Yes, if convenient.
Soil mix: All-purpose.
Soil moisture: Evenly moist to on the dry side.
Propagation: Tip cuttings.
Problems: Hoya is virtually trouble-free.
Comments: Tip cuttings of hoya placed in a glass or vase of water will root and grow there for months; maintain the water level and once a month pour out all the old and replace with fresh.

OCIMUM

Pronunciation: OH-sim-um
Common name: Basil
Uses: Sill.
Leaf color: Green or purple.
Flowers: White, but insignificant.

ENVIRONMENTAL NEEDS:
Light: Sunny east, south, or west window; thrives in a fluorescent-light garden.
Temperature: 62-75 degrees F.
Humidity: Medium.
Mist frequently: Yes, if convenient.
Soil mix: All-purpose.
Soil moisture: Evenly moist.
Propagation: Grow from seeds.
Problems: Mealybugs may attack basil.
Comments: Frequent pinching back helps encourage compact, full growth; use the pinchings for seasoning. Discard old plants and start over with seedlings every six months.

OXALIS

Pronunciation: OX-uh-liss
Common name: Oxalis
Uses: Desk top, sill, hanging basket, pedestal.
Leaf color: Green or green and yellow.
Flowers: White, pink.

ENVIRONMENTAL NEEDS:
Light: Sunny east, south, or west window; thrives in a fluorescent-light garden.
Temperature: 62-75 degrees F.
Humidity: Medium.
Mist frequently: Yes, if convenient.
Soil mix: All-purpose.
Soil moisture: Evenly moist.
Propagation: By division.
Problems: Red spider mites may attack if air is hot, dry and stale; watch for mealybugs.
Comments: There are many kinds of oxalis in cultivation, but the three most easily cultivated as all-year house plants are *O. rubra* (sometimes listed as *O. crassipes;* green leaves, rose-pink flowers), *O. regnellii* (olive-green leaves, white flowers) and *O. martiana aureo-reticulata* (green leaves veined with yellow, pink flowers). These are seldom seen in local plant shops but they are available by mail from such specialists as Logees and Merry Gardens.

PANDANUS

Pronunciation: pan-DAY-nus
Common name: Screw pine
Uses: Floor shrub, hanging basket, or pedestal.
Leaf color: Green and white.
Flowers: No.

ENVIRONMENTAL NEEDS:
Light: Near a sunny east, south, or west window; tolerates
 long periods in bright light with little or no direct sun.
Temperature: 62-75 degrees F.
Humidity: Medium; tolerates less.
Mist frequently: Yes, if convenient.
Soil mix: All-purpose.
Soil moisture: Evenly moist to on the dry side.
Propagation: By removing offsets.
Problems: In hot, dry, stale air, red spider mites may attack.
 Severely dry soil may cause leaf tips to die.
Comments: A well-grown, symmetrical screw pine makes a
 stunning plant to display on a pedestal, but there are sharp
 spines along the leaf edges, so be sure to position it where
 no one is likely to brush against the plant.

PLECTRANTHUS

Pronunciation: pleck-TRANTH-us
Common name: Swedish ivy
Uses: Hanging basket or pedestal.
Leaf color: Green or green and white.
Flowers: No.

ENVIRONMENTAL NEEDS:

Light: In or near a sunny east, south, or west window; adapts to less light, but leaves and stems may be spindly; young plants thrive in a fluorescent-light garden.

Temperature: 62-75 degrees F.

Humidity: Medium; tolerates less.

Mist frequently: Yes, if convenient.

Soil mix: All-purpose.

Soil moisture: Evenly moist.

Propagation: Tip cuttings.

Problems: Relatively trouble-free. Severely dry soil causes all the older leaves to wither and die quickly.

Comments: Swedish ivy is one of the best all-around house plants. If the soil is never allowed to dry out, it is surprisingly tolerant of drafts of hot air, for example when it is hung in a window over a heating unit. To encourage full, compact growth, pinch back frequently. When stems near the base become woody and leafless, it is time to start new plants from tip cuttings.

PLEOMELE

Pronunciation: plee-OH-may-lee
Common name: Pleomele
Uses: Desk top, sill, floor shrub, tree effect, or pedestal.
Leaf color: Green.
Flowers: White, but rare as a house plant.

ENVIRONMENTAL NEEDS:
Light: Bright light but not more than an hour or two of sun
   shining directly on the leaves.
Temperature: 62-75 degrees F.
Humidity: Medium; tolerates less.
Mist frequently: Yes, if convenient.
Soil mix: All-purpose.
Soil moisture: Evenly moist to wet.
Propagation: Tip cuttings.
Problems: Severely dry soil causes the leaf tips to turn brown
   and die. A remarkably trouble-free plant.
Comments: Specimen pleomeles as much as eight feet tall and
   four feet across are occasionally available; one of these, when
   dramatically lighted at night, makes a beautiful living sculp-
   ture.

SAINTPAULIA

Pronunciation: saint-PAUL-ee-uh
Common name: African violet.
Uses: Desk top, sill, hanging basket, pedestal, terrarium.
Leaf color: Green or green and white.
Flowers: White, blue, lavender, purple, pink, wine-red.

ENVIRONMENTAL NEEDS:
Light: Bright light or near a sunny east, south, or west window; thrives in a fluorescent-light garden.
Temperature: 62-75 degrees F.
Humidity: Medium.
Mist frequently: No.
Soil mix: African violet.
Soil moisture: Evenly moist.
Propagation: By division or leaf cuttings.
Problems: Mealybugs and cyclamen mites favor African violets. Watering the roots with cold water, or splashing the leaves with it, causes yellow spots to form. Severely dry soil causes older leaves, as well as developing flower buds, to wilt and die. Too much hot sun shining directly on the leaves will burn spots in them; lack of light results in pale leaves on long, spindly stems and prevents flowering.
Comments: Hybrid African violets available by mail from specialists come in hundreds of different varieties.

SANSEVIERIA

Pronunciation: san-zuh-VEER-ee-uh
Common name: Snake plant, mother-in-law's tongue.
Uses: Desk top, sill, pedestal.
Leaf Color: Green, silver, gold.
Flowers: White and fragrant, but rare.

ENVIRONMENTAL NEEDS:
Light: Thrives in a range between low light and a sunny south
    window; grows well in artificial light.
Temperature: 62-75 degrees F.
Humidity: Low.
Mist frequently: No.
Soil mix: All-purpose.
Soil moisture: Evenly moist to on the dry side.
Propagation: By division.
Problems: None.
Comments: Sansevierias are absolutely fail-safe house plants.
    Specialists offer unusual kinds seldom seen in local shops.

SCILLA

Pronunciation: SILL-uh
Common name: S. *violacea* is sometimes called silver squill.
Uses: Desk top, sill, hanging basket, or terrarium.
Leaf color: Olive green, silver, burgundy.
Flowers: White to pale lavender, but relatively insignificant.

ENVIRONMENTAL NEEDS:

Light: In or near a sunny east, south, or west window; thrives in a fluorescent-light garden.
Temperature: 62-72 degrees F.
Humidity: Medium; tolerates less.
Mist frequently: No.
Soil mix: All-purpose.
Soil moisture: Evenly moist.
Propagation: By division.
Problems: Mostly trouble-free. Severely dry soil will cause older leaves to turn yellow and die, but this plant grows from a succulent bulb and can survive considerable neglect and lack of water.
Comments: A beautiful, small-foliage house plant that is very easy to grow. If you can't find it locally, order it from a specialist.

SPATHIPHYLLUM

Pronunciation: spath-if-FILL-um
Common name: Peace lily.
Uses: Desk top or sill if small; floor shrub or plant pedestal if large.
Leaf color: Green.
Flowers: White.

ENVIRONMENTAL NEEDS:
Light: Bright light, preferably near a sunny east, south, or west window, but placed so that little or no hot sun shines directly on the leaves.
Temperature: 62-75 degrees F.
Humidity: Medium; tolerates less.
Mist frequently: Yes, if convenient.
Soil mix: All-purpose.
Soil moisture: Evenly moist to wet.
Propagation: By division.
Problems: Severely dry soil causes the leaf tips to turn brown and die. Virtually pest-free.
Comments: One of the most durable and rewarding of all medium-size foliage plants, with the added bonus of flowers off and on through the year. Some varieties grow only about eighteen inches tall, others reach up to four feet.

TRADESCANTIA

Pronunciation: tradd-ess-KANT-ee-uh
Common name: Wandering Jew.
Uses: Hanging basket or pedestal.
Leaf color: Green, white, purple, silver.
Flowers: Occasionally, but insignificant.

ENVIRONMENTAL NEEDS:
Light: In or near a sunny east, south, or west window; insufficient light results in spindly, pale growth.
Temperature: 62-75 degrees F.
Humidity: Medium; tolerates less.
Mist frequently: Yes, if convenient.
Soil mix: All-purpose.
Soil moisture: Evenly moist.
Propagation: Tip cuttings.
Problems: Severely dry soil causes old leaves as well as the tips of younger ones to die. Roots and lower stems may rot if the soil is soggy wet and poorly drained for long periods of time. Frequent pinching back is necessary to encourage full, compact growth.
Comments: Plain green tradescantias seem to tolerate low light better than the other kinds.

By-Mail Sources for Plants, Supplies, and Equipment

Although local nurseries, shops, and garden centers carry a wide variety of plants, and supplies needed for their care, one of the most exciting aspects of gardening is reading and dreaming over the catalogs of mail-order specialists. These offer a ready, convenient source for virtually every plant in cultivation, plus highly specialized tools, equipment, and supplies.

The list that follows is by no means all-inclusive; inclusion is no more an endorsement than exclusion is condemnation. Over the years I have purchased plants and other materials from most of these firms and have almost always been pleased. I have also had the pleasure of visiting many of the nurseries and greenhouses listed, an experience I highly recommend.

ABBEY GARDEN, 176 Toro Canyon Road, Carpinteria, California 93013. Cacti and other succulents; 50 cents for catalog.

ABBOT'S NURSERY, Route 4, Box 482, Mobile, Alabama 36609. Camellias.

ALBERTS & MERKEL BROTHERS, INC., 2210 S. Federal Highway, Boynton Beach, Florida 33435. Orchids, tropical foliage and flowering plants; 25 cents for list.

ANTONELLI BROTHERS, 2545 Capitola Road, Santa Cruz, California 95060. Tuberous begonias, gloxinias, achimenes.

LOUISE BARNABY, 12178 Highview Street, Vicksburg, Michigan 49097. African violets; send stamp for list.

MRS. MARY V. BOOSE, 9 Turney Place, Trumbull, Connecticut 06611. African violets and episcias; 15 cents for list.

JOHN BRUDY'S RARE PLANT HOUSE, P.O. Box 1348, Cocoa Beach, Florida 32931. Unusual seeds and plants; $1 for catalog.

BUELL'S GREENHOUSES, Weeks Road, Eastford, Connecticut 06242. Complete listing of gloxinias, African violets, and other gesneriads; supplies; $1 for catalog.

BURGESS SEED AND PLANT COMPANY, 67 East Battle Creek, Galesburg, Michigan 49053. Plants, bulbs, seeds.

W. ATLEE BURPEE COMPANY, Warminster, Pennsylvania 18974. Seeds, bulbs, plants; supplies.

DAVID BUTTRAM, P.O. Box 193, Independence, Missouri 64051. African violets; 10 cents for list.

CACTUS GEM NURSERY, 10092 Mann Drive, Cupertino, California (visit Thursday-Sunday); by mail write P.O. Box 327, Aromas, California 95004.

CASTLE VIOLETS, 614 Castle Road, Colorado Springs, Colorado 80904. African violets.

CHAMPION'S AFRICAN VIOLETS, 8848 Van Hoesen Road, Clay, New York 13041. African violets; send stamp for list.

VICTOR CONSTANTINOV, 3321 21st Street, Apt. 7, San Francisco, California 94110. African violets, columneas, and episcias; send stamp for list.

COOK'S GERANIUM NURSERY, 714 N. Grand, Lyons, Kansas 67544. Geraniums; 25 cents for catalog.

DAVIS CACTUS GARDEN, 1522 Jefferson Street, Kerrville, Texas 78028. 25 cents for catalog.

DEGIORGI COMPANY, INC., Council Bluffs, Iowa 51504. Seeds and bulbs.

P. DE JAGER AND SONS, 188 Asbury Street, South Hamilton, Massachusetts 01982. Bulbs.

L. EASTERBROOK GREENHOUSES, 10 Craig Street, Butler, Ohio 44822. African violets, other gesneriads, terrarium plants; supplies; 75 cents for catalog.

ELECTRIC FARM, 104 B Lee Road, Oak Hill, New York 12460. Gesneriads; send self-addressed stamped envelope for list.

FARMER SEED AND NURSERY COMPANY, Faribault, Minnesota 55021. Seeds, bulbs, plants.

FENNELL ORCHID COMPANY, INC., 26715 S. W. 157th Avenue, Homestead, Florida 33030. Orchids; supplies.

FERNWOOD PLANTS, 1311 Fernwood Pacific Drive, Topanga, California 90290. Rare and unusual cacti.

FFOULKES, 610 Bryan Street, Jacksonville, Florida 32202. African violets; 25 cents for list.

HENRY FIELD SEED & NURSERY COMPANY, 407 Sycamore, Shenandoah, Iowa 51601. Plants, bulbs, seeds; supplies.

FISCHER GREENHOUSES, Linwood, New Jersey 08221. African violets and other gesneriads; 25 cents for catalog.

FOX ORCHIDS, 6615 W. Markham, Little Rock, Arkansas 72205. Orchids; supplies.

ARTHUR FREED ORCHIDS, INC., 5731 S. Bonsall Drive, Malibu, California 90265. Orchids; supplies.

J. HOWARD FRENCH, P.O. Box 87, Center Rutland, Vermont 05736. Bulbs.

GIRARD NURSERIES, P.O. Box 428, Geneva, Ohio 44041. Bonsai materials.

GRIGSBY CACTUS GARDENS, 2354 Bella Vista Drive, Vista, California 92083. Cacti and other succulents; 50 cents for catalog.

GURNEY SEED AND NURSERY COMPANY, Yankton, South Dakota 57078. Seeds, bulbs, plants.

ORCHIDS BY HAUSERMANN, INC., P.O. Box 363, Elmhurst, Illinois 60126. Orchids; supplies; $1.25 for catalog.

HELEN'S CACTUS, 2205 Mirasol, Brownsville, Texas 78520. Cacti and other succulents; 10 cents for list.

HENRIETTA'S NURSERY, 1345 N. Brawley Avenue, Fresno, California 93705. Cacti and other succulents; 20 cents for catalog.

HILLTOP FARM, Route 3, Box 216, Cleveland, Texas. Geraniums and herbs.

SIM T. HOLMES, 100 Tustarawas Road, Beaver, Pennsylvania 15009. African violets, miniature and regular.

SPENCER M. HOWARD ORCHID IMPORTS, 11802 Huston Street, North Hollywood, California 91607. Unusual orchids.

GORDON M. HOYT ORCHIDS, Seattle Heights, Washington 98036. Orchids; supplies.

MARGARET ILGENFRITZ ORCHIDS, Blossom Lane, P.O. Box 665, Monroe, Michigan. Orchids; supplies; $1 for catalog.

JONES AND SCULLY, 2200 N.W. 33rd Avenue, Miami, Florida 33142. Orchids and supplies; $3.50 for catalog.

KARTUZ GREENHOUSES, 92 Chestnut Street, Wilmington, Massachusetts 01887. Gesneriads, begonias, house plants in general; supplies; 50 cents for catalog.

KIRKPATRICK'S, 27785 De Anza Street, Barstow, California 92311. Cacti and other succulents; 10 cents for list.

KOLB'S GREENHOUSES, 725 Belvedere Road, Phillipsburg, New Jersey 08865. African violets; send stamp for list.

LAURAY, Undermountain Road, Route 41, Salisbury, Connecticut 06068. Gesneriads, cacti and other succulents, begonias; 50 cents for catalog.

LOGEE'S GREENHOUSES, 55 North Street, Danielson, Connecticut 06239. Complete selection of house plants, with special emphasis on begonias and geraniums; $1 for catalog.

LYNDON LYON, 14 Mutchler Street, Dolgeville, New York 13329. African violets and other gesneriads.

MARY'S AFRICAN VIOLETS, 19788 San Juan, Detroit, Michigan 48221. African violets; supplies.

EARL MAY SEED & NURSERY COMPANY, Shenandoah, Iowa 51603. Seeds, bulbs, plants.

Rod McLellan Company, 1450 El Camino Real, South San Francisco, California 94080. Orchids; supplies.

Merry Gardens, Camden, Maine 04843. House plants and herbs; large selection of begonias and geraniums; $1 for catalog.

Mini-Roses, P.O. Box 245, Station A, Dallas, Texas 75208. Miniature roses.

Modlin's Cactus Gardens, Route 4, Box 3034, Vista, California 92083. Cacti and other succulents; 25 cents for catalog.

Cactus by Mueller, 10411 Rosedale Highway, Bakersfield, California 93308. Cacti and other succulents; 10 cents for list.

Nuccio's Nurseries, 3555 Chaney Trail, Altadena, California 91001. Hybrid camellias and azaleas.

Orinda Nursery, Bridgeville, Delaware 19933. Hybrid camellias.

George W. Park Seed Company, Inc., Greenwood, South Carolina 29647. Seeds, bulbs, plants; supplies.

Penn Valley Orchids, 239 Old Gulph Road, Wynnewood, Pennsylvania 19096. Orchids.

John Scheepers, Inc., 63 Wall Street, New York, 10005. Flowering bulbs.

Sequoia Nursery, 2519 East Noble Street, Visalia, California 93277. Miniature roses.

Shaffer's Tropical Gardens, Inc., 3220 41 Avenue, Capitola, California 95010. Orchids.

P. R. Sharp, 104 N. Chapel Avenue, #3, Alhambra, California 91801. South American and Mexican cacti.

R. H. Shumway Seedsman, Rockford, Illinois 61101. Seeds, plants, bulbs.

Singers' Growing Things, 6385 Enfield Avenue, Reseda, California 91335. Succulents.

SMITH'S CACTUS GARDEN, P.O. Box 871, Paramount, California 90723. Cacti and other succulents; 30 cents for list.

FRED A. STEWART, INC., Orchids, 1212 East Las Tunas Drive, San Gabriel, California 91778. Orchids; supplies.

STOKES SEEDS, 737 Main Street, Buffalo, New York 14203. Seeds.

ED STORMS, 4223 Pershing, Fort Worth, Texas 76107. Lithops and other succulents.

SUNNYBROOK FARMS, 9448 Mayfield Road, Chesterland, Ohio 44026. Herbs, scented geraniums, many other plants.

SUNNYSLOPE GARDENS, 8638 Huntington Drive, San Gabriel, California 91775. Chrysanthemums.

THOMPSON & MORGAN, INC., P.O. Box 24, Somerdale, New Jersey 08083. Seeds of many unusual plants.

THON'S GARDEN MUMS, 4815 Oak Street, Crystal Lake, Illinois 60014. Chrysanthemums.

TINARI GREENHOUSES, Box 190, 2325 Valley Road, Huntingdon Valley, Pennsylvania 19006. African violets, gesneriads; supplies; 25 cents for catalog.

WHITE FLOWER FARM, Litchfield, Connecticut 06759. Spectacular English hybrid tuberous-rooted begonias; other plants and bulbs.

WILSON BROTHERS, Roachdale, Indiana 47121. House plants, with special emphasis on geraniums.

12 ❦ Plant People and Plant Careers

❦ Career opportunities in horticulture have increased dramatically in recent years, not only in the agricultural industry that feeds and clothes us, and in the horticultural therapy described in Chapter 9, but with plants in general. All the individuals whose stories are told here have elected to live and work with plants either as a career or as a serious avocation.

The first seven are considered together because all the interviews were conducted by telephone in a single evening. At the time of my call, the moonlight was bright enough for Carolyn Busch to see and smell every fragrant flower growing in her New York loft. Uptown, Dean Doss was checking for healthy root systems on spring bulbs he was forcing for winter bloom, and in the same apartment Octavio Figueroa was clipping miniature lawns of baby's-tears. In Philadelphia, Ernesta and Fred Ballard had eaten dinner hastily to have more time to relax with their plants. And in Ohio, Tony Badalamenti and Don Vanderbrook were ignoring the first frost outdoors by poring over seed catalogs, making plans for keeping their garden room in bloom.

What these seven gardeners have in common are rooms designed for peaceful coexistence between plants and people. All of them not only grow plants well but display them with respect. At the thought of turning an entire room into a place for living with plants, one anticipates that plants will surely grow better grouped together, and that at the same time they'll have to be displayed so that each can be appreciated. A garden room is definitely a good idea if there is bright light all day in winter, or, preferably, half a day of direct sun. It helps if the air is pleasantly cool and circulates freely, wafting 40 to 50 percent humidity. It helps too if the floor and walls can be drenched with the hose while watering the plants with tepid water. And, of course, you should be devoted to your plants. But none of these prescriptions carries the clout of having plenty of sunlight in winter, unless you elect to depend on supplementary artificial light.

The final success with a garden room is something that grows with your own sophistication as a gardener. At the beginning you may rejoice in a roomful of almost any kind of greenery, but soon you're ready for adventure. Perhaps an orchid, or a bromeliad. In no time it will be you instead of Carolyn Busch who says, "I was tired of scheffleras. I knew there had to be something more interesting."

While an art student in Philadelphia, Carolyn Busch accepted two cuttings from a friend. Before she knew it her windows were filled. "It was fantastic—my plants were better than those I saw in shops." Next stop New York, and Carolyn was seriously into Greenleaves, her own plant business. Today her natural affinity for growing things is supplemented by years of experience. She's observant about the peculiar needs of every plant. "If a plant's moisture needs are critical, I keep a record of how much and when I've watered it." Carolyn mists foliage daily and about once a month adds Dr. Bronner's Peppermint Soap (from a health food store) to the mister. "This dissolves grime and chases insects. It washes off quickly when you faithfully mist every day with clean water."

Fred and Ernesta Ballard maintain long and lasting relationships with their plants. The gardenia bonsai they display on a table in the entryway was a twenty-five-cent rooted cutting when it came to live with them more than twenty years ago. An ancient Ponderosa lemon tree in the dining room has also been painstakingly trained in the manner of a bonsai. Even demure rosemary, "for remembrance," has been sheared into stylish topiary trees. Ernesta recalls, "I was young when we married. Soon there were four children with a mother who had no education for any outside pursuit. Plants seemed like a good thing to get into." Two and a half years later Ernesta graduated from the Pennsylvania School of Horticulture for Women (now coeducational and known as the Ambler Campus of Temple University) and opened a retail nursery that she operated until 1963, when she became executive secretary of the Pennsylvania Horticultural Society. Since the 1960s, she has, with quiet determination, inspired thousands of people to garden.

Dean Doss grew up in Virginia surrounded by seasonal flowers, while Octavio Figueroa's childhood playground was a leafy rain forest. The fountain in their living room was designed and built by Octavio, an architect, to give the "soothing sound of splashing water." The materials he used were poured concrete with vermiculite (to make it lighter weight) and a recirculating pump. Clay saucers hold perfectly sculpted domes of baby's-tears. Incandescents and fluorescents burn twelve hours a day to supplement natural light. Dean practices his specialty of coaxing winter bloom from spring flowers in a bedroom window fitted with louvered doors. "When these are closed, the sill space between them and the glass provides a cool place for tulip, daffodil, and hyacinth bulbs to take root." Octavio says that plants "make life bearable in the asphalt jungle," and Dean adds, "You might say we share a garden, not an apartment."

In Ohio, Tony Badalamenti and Don Vanderbrook have carried a love of nature and outdoor plants into their garden room, which they resurrected from the ruins of Chagrin Falls's oldest gasoline station and garage. Acrylic plastic sheeting replaced the original roof. Tony built treillage to decorate and detail the walls and roof, and Don found clay tile from Mexico for the floor. The room is an ever changing garden of such specialties as hanging nasturtiums, azalea trees, potted clumps of Enchantment lilies, Iceland poppies, primroses, and ever-blooming begonias.

An encouraging fact for any yet-to-be gardener is that each of these seven gardeners began with a single plant. Involvement followed. Now, when asked, "If you could travel anywhere on a vacation, what would you do?" the response was invariable: "Visit other gardeners, see what they grow and share plant experiences."

The following stories of eleven more plant people I want to tell individually, since each has a full-time professional commitment to horticulture and a specialized area of expertise which, like most gardeners, all of them share freely with anyone who asks.

Marc Cathey, as head of ornamentals investigation for the United States Department of Agriculture, with headquarters in Beltsville, Maryland, supervises programs aimed at solving real problems for amateur as well as commercial growers. His specialties include plant genetics and breeding, plant physiology, entomology, botany, and phytoillumination (the growing of plants by means of artificial light).

To get started with house plants, Dr. Cathey suggests growing in water. "You can use any vase, beverage bottle, aquarium, even an old canning jar." Plants he recommends include geranium, peperomia, aluminum plant, impatiens, begonia, hibiscus, coleus, aucuba, English ivy, hoya, Chinese evergreen, plectranthus, and grape ivy. Make cuttings of healthy growth. Remove any leaves along the lower stem that will be in the water, then arrange the cuttings loosely in the container. Before using any container, wash it in warm, soapy water. Rinse, dry, then fill with fresh water. Also wash and rinse the plant material; this removes pests.

In the Cathey home, one window is filled with old, new, unusual, and colored bottles filled with water and with thriving rooted cuttings. This is the kind of gardening experience Dr. Cathey champions, because it can be done by anyone under almost any circumstance. "All you have to do is add water to replace that lost by evaporation." For best long-term results, he also advises that water be replaced once a month to control algae and that a water-soluble house-plant fertilizer be added to the water at one-fourth to one-fifth the rate recommended by the manufacturer for potted plants; use a measuring spoon.

Carol Adler is quite simply mad for plants. At her shop in a leading department store, plant parenthood is not taken casually. You are allowed to buy what she feels you can succeed with, and certain plants are her pets, not for sale to anyone. "I want people to understand I really love plants." And love them she does, all over the store, in her apartment, and in the country. She has switched the entire store to live plant materials. Best-lasting in dim light are dracaenas Janet Craig and *marginata* and palms. She prefers the kentia, but is forced to use arecas because of their availability ("Just be sure the soil in which an areca is growing *never* dries out").

Advice from Carol has the unmistakable ring of real experience. On clay pots: "These drink water the same as soil. Once every two weeks submerge the entire pot in water for fifteen minutes."

On soil: "Most packaged potting soils need perlite and vermiculite added to them. Experiment, the same as you do with cooking. At home I spread an old shower curtain on the kitchen table and mix my potting soil. It's really fun." On soil pH: "Except for gardenia, azalea, and citrus, most house plants need a sweet soil. Spider plant is especially sensitive. The symptom is a black strip down the leaves. The cure is to scratch a teaspoon or two of agricultural limestone into the soil. Also cultivate surface soil in pots just as you would outdoors. All you need is a kitchen fork."

On ventilation: "People who buy plants for the first time seem to think they have to keep the windows closed. When the weather is warm, keep windows open part of the time. It's a fantastic experience for potted plants."

On buying: "Avoid bargains. There are none. Never buy from a store that keeps plants on the sidewalk in near-freezing weather. This puts tropicals in terminal shock, and after you've brought them home with high hopes they slowly die, a very depressing experience."

On humidity: "Set pots in saucers or trays with wood chips in the bottom. Add water to the chips, but not enough to touch the pot bases. Containers of fresh water sitting among your plants also evaporate moisture into the air."

On decorating: "Clay pot saucers sweat. Buy a piece of cork and cut it to fit underneath, otherwise moisture seepage will ruin floors and carpeting."

On favorite plants: "Try something besides grape ivy and philodendron. Be adventuresome. Polypodium and davallia ferns are terrific, also hundreds of different begonias."

A few years ago Allan and Marcia Schulte adopted a huge jade plant that they named Jason. Before they knew it, Allan had given up brokering, Marcia had given up teaching, and they had opened a little plant shop. It grew, divided, and now there is a third, all three in Cleveland, all called Big Plants Unlimited. What tree-size house plants do they recommend? *"Ficus benjamina,* weeping fig, is the most disease-resistant. Big, old dizygothecas are easy; the young ones are difficult. Among palms, kentias are favored but hard to find. We love beaucarnea, or ponytail, and *Pleomele reflexa* trained as tree standards; both look African. One of the few really big plants that requires little light is *Dracaena fragrans,* variety *massangeana."*

To keep foliage clean, the Schultes advise taking a damp cloth or small sponge in each hand. Sandwich the leaves between. "This is quick and effective, the way we do it in the stores." To clean the small leaves of *Ficus benjamina,* put it outdoors in a warm rain.

What plants are good if you don't have much light? "Any Chinese evergreen or aglaonema. Aspidistra will grow in near darkness. *Spathiphyllum clevelandi* and *Dracaena marginata,* our most popular plant, also survive poor light. At home we have a nine-foot rhapis palm sustained by two Cool-Beam incandescent floodlights positioned about four feet away and burned ten to twelve hours daily."

What about bugs? "Zectran solves most problems. For red spider mites, spray alternately with Kelthane and Dimite. Use misters and mix your own pesticide."

Purely for fun, Marcia Schulte collects miniature ferns, which she keeps in a kitchen window, and Allan has various polyscias planted in Chinese pots. Without much age or training, they appear to be ancient bonsai.

The Schultes' story is not unlike that of another friend, Bagley Reid, who left Wall Street to satisfy a lifetime desire to open his own landscaping and plant-maintenance business. The stock market was bad in March of 1974 when Bagley decided to start a business that was based less on competition than advising people about the stock market is. Bagley has learned that people are serious about plants and listen more readily to a plant expert's advice than to that of a stock broker; they will take instructions on plant care but be skeptical about stock-market advice. He has found that he prefers this combination of noncompetitiveness and credibility, and he now spends most of his time in the country working with plants.

Sandra Mauro was out for a weekend drive a few years ago when she noticed signs announcing a flower show. She stopped, she looked, she was amazed. She brought her husband, Albert, back, and although neither had gardened before, Sandra now has an embarrassment of blue ribbons and he has served as president of the Garden Center Association of Kansas City.

Growing plants indoors is an even more recent experience for Sandra. "I was awed by the idea of being totally responsible for a plant, but then Albert gave me a twelve-by-twelve-foot greenhouse and I was into it seriously. Now our children are too, especially Maria. When I go plant hunting she gives her allowance to me so I can pick out something special. Her pet is the mother fern, *Asplenium bulbiferum*. She cuts the bulbils off the leaves and sells them to me for a quarter each. These are great for terrarium planting, where they root and grow."

Sandra teaches horticulture to six classes of children yearly: "First I take them into the greenhouse and show and talk about some of the more unusual plants, like the rosary vine. They feel, squeeze, smell, and finally pick out what they want. Cuttings may already be rooted, or I teach them how to make new ones."

Terrariums are Sandra's specialty. "I use jars I can reach into, so it is a real gardening experience. For children, large pickle jars from a drive-in or a hospital kitchen are perfect. To plant, first add a thick layer of charcoal chips in the bottom, then the growing medium." Sandra uses the Missouri Botanic Garden mix, made according to this recipe: three parts black peat moss, one part pasteurized soil, one part vermiculite. To each gallon of mix add one-fourth cup bone meal. Moisten. Put in a plastic bag and let cure for four to five weeks, at which time it will have reached a high level of biological activity and is ideal for planting.

"For upright terrarium plants I like boxwood and dwarf euonymus. They grow slowly and are amenable to trimming. To use small-leaved English ivies like Hahn's, Needlepoint, *scutifolia,* and *conglomerata,* simply make cuttings and insert them, unrooted, in the terrarium." Sandra also recommends any small fern, miniature gloxinias, selaginellas, strawberry-geranium, earth star bromeliads (cryptanthus), and miniature rex begonias.

General planting advice for terrariums: "Make natural landscapes with hills and valleys. Don't jam the container with plants. Allow contrast in scale; leave open spaces. Create a scene in miniature, true to nature. As plants grow, clip off any excessive growth. Also promptly remove any yellowing or dead leaves and spent flowers. Terrariums need bright or reflected light, but little or no direct sun striking them."

Michael Kartuz studied music theory and composition at New York University, all the while hybridizing gloxinias, African violets, and begonias at home. After graduation he spent ten years working for an oil company, then decided that plants were really his métier. He moved to Wilmington, Massachusetts, and since then the plants, as well as the Kartuz greenhouses, have been on the increase. Now his green thumbs never touch the ivories, but he plays recorded music in the greenhouses and says, quite emphatically, "Music makes plants grow."

The best flowering plant for houses and apartments? "The African violet. There are thousands of varieties. If one doesn't do well, try another." The related columneas are equally outstanding, he says. "New hybrids bloom nonstop, lining short, bushy, or cascading stems with pink, rose, red, or yellow flowers." Some of Michael's own columnea hybrids are ranked among the best: Magic Lantern, Mary Ann, Ramadan, Robin, Sylvia, and Yellow Hammer.

Michael grows everything in a soilless mix prepared according to this recipe: two quarts sphagnum peat moss, screened; one quart Terralite vermiculite; one quart coarse perlite; one tablespoon ground limestone. Use Canadian or European peat moss, which should be rubbed through a half-inch-mesh hardware cloth sieve to remove lumps and small twigs. Put all ingredients in a suitable container and mix well. The mix can be used at once or stored indefinitely. Moisten it before use. Feed lightly but frequently. This soilless mix can be used for any potted plant. Ingredients are lightweight and easily found in local shops.

Waldo Donaho, a professional grower at Burton Flower and Garden, Burton, Ohio, thirty miles east of Cleveland, began with ten plants in hanging baskets in 1958. Now he has tens of thousands of house-plant baskets, not to mention thousands more for outdoors.

Waldo is willing to try any plant in a basket. If it does well under greenhouse conditions, he gives it the acid test as a house plant before it goes into production. Flowering hanging baskets he recommends include columneas Early Bird and Firebird, the small angel-wing begonias, Polka Dot vinca ("This flowered all last summer in a north-facing window of an office here"), hypocyrta or goldfish plant, and variegated flowering maple. For foliage baskets he first suggests succulents, including sedum (especially a hybrid form of burro's-tail), trailing echeveria, Oscularia deltoides, string of pearls, rhipsalis, kalanchoe, and peanut cactus. Among leafy basket plants Waldo prefers wandering Jew ("Purple-and-silver zebrina for sun, the one with white-striped green leaves for shade"). For a small basket, try English baby's-tears (*Pilea depressa*). Cape ivy (a senecio) he finds impossible to kill in sun or shade. Also highly rated: any Swedish ivy, rabbit's-foot fern, grape ivy, kangaroo vine, and spider plant ("The leaf tips die back every time it dries out severely"). What to plant in? "A soilless medium such as Jiffy-Mix. Feed, water, trim back regularly."

George and Virginie Elbert offer proof in their New York apartment that almost anything can be grown indoors and under fluorescent light. George, a past president of the Indoor Light Gardening Society, is one of today's most articulate spokespersons for raising plants without natural light and is the author of *The Indoor Light Gardening Book;* together he and Virginie have written several books, including *Fun with Terrarium Gardening* and *Fun with Growing Herbs Indoors.*

The Elberts say that to grow plants under fluorescent light an excellent combination is one Warm White with one Cool White tube; no supplementary incandescent is recommended. To augment natural light for large house plants or trees use Cool Beam or Cool-Lux incandescent floodlights in ceramic sockets. These are available in sizes from 75 to 150 watts, sometimes up to 300 watts, and can be burned six to twelve hours out of every twenty-four.

All the Elberts' plant lights are on timers, set for sixteen-hour days, although they have experimented with twelve- and fourteen-hour periods and see little difference. To get started, the Elberts recommend one unit with two tubes, either 20 or 40 watt, placed about twenty inches above a table or shelf, or even under a coffee table or kitchen cabinet or in a fireplace. In their fireplace, in one fish-tank terrarium under two 20-watt fluorescents, they grow fittonia, rex begonia, selaginella, *Peperomia puteolata,* a small fern, and, for flowers, episcia, crape-myrtlette, and *Gesneria cuneifolia.* In another light setup they have the

Kartuz hybrid gesneria Lemon Drop, which has bloomed non-stop for three years. The Elberts grow a remarkable variety of plants under fluorescents, including carissa, malpighia, and portulacaria as bonsai; cacti from seeds; *Anthurium crystallinum,* flowering allophyton, cuphea, hoya, jacobinia, seemania, crossandra, miniature gloxinia, hypocyrta, Moon Chimes abutilon, exacum; and many fragrant herbs.

"Watching plants grow and being responsible for them provides us with thinking time," Virginie says. "It's never more useful than while we are in the midst of writing a book. Neither of us could imagine living without plants."

Perhaps one great appeal of horticulture as a career is that practical experience can carry as much weight as that of a formal education, sometimes even more. A nationwide horticultural certification program, initiated by the American Horticultural Society, awards an "American Diploma in Horticulture" to applicants who meet prescribed standards for demonstrating art and skill in horticultural practices. The program was not conceived to compete with degree training in schools and colleges, where the emphasis is more academic. It is primarily concerned with the use of practical gardening skills. For complete information write to the American Horticultural Society, Mount Vernon, Virginia 22121.

Courses in plant care are now offered by every local horticultural organization and botanical garden, and by many Y's, colleges, and universities. Institutions in the United States and Canada that offer horticulture as a major field for baccalaureate or advanced degrees, as well as those that offer training below the baccalaureate level, are listed below. The code letters are B (Bachelor), M (Master's), P (Ph.D.), AAS (Associate in Applied Science), AS (Associate in Science), AA (Associate in Arts), T (credits are transferable), N (credits are nontransferable), C (certificate), D (diploma), CC (correspondence courses), WS (work-study).

The range of horticulture specialization is wide and varies considerably among these schools. For detailed information write to the Director of Admissions of the college or university being considered. Several institutions offer landscape architecture; a list of those accredited by the American Society of Landscape Architects is available from ASLA, 1750 Old Meadow Road, McLean, Virginia 22101.

Alabama

Alabama A & M University
Department of Natural Resource & Environmental Studies
Normal, Alabama 35762
B, M, T

Arizona

Arizona State University
Department of Horticulture
Tempe, Arizona 85281
B, M, T, D

University of Arizona
Department of Horticulture & Landscape Architecture
Tucson, Arizona 85721
B, M, P, T, D

Arkansas

Arkansas State University
Department of Horticulture

State University, Arkansas 72467
B

Petite Jean Vocational-Technical School
Highway 9 North
Morilton, Arkansas 72110
M

University of Arkansas
Department of Horticulture
Fayetteville, Arkansas 72701
B, M

California

California State Polytechnic University
Department of Horticulture
San Luis Obispo, California 93501
B, AAS, T, C, D

California State Polytechnic University
Ornamental Horticulture Department
Pomona, California 91768
B

California State University
Department of Horticulture
Chico, California 95926
B, M, T

California State University
Department of Horticulture
Fresno, California 93710
B, M, T, D

University of California
Department of Plant Sciences
Riverside, California 92502
B, M, P, T, D

University of California
Department of Population & Environmental Biology
Irvine, California 92664
B, M, P

University of California
Environmental Horticulture Dept.
Davis, California 95616
B, M, P, T, D

Colorado

Colorado State University
Department of Horticulture
Fort Collins, Colorado 80521
B, M, P

Connecticut

University of Connecticut
Plant Science Department
Horticulture Section
Storrs, Connecticut 06268
B, M, P, D, C

Delaware

University of Delaware
Department of Horticulture
School of Agricultural Sciences
Newark, Delaware 19711
B, M, P, AAS, AS, T

Florida

Florida Southern College
Citrus Institute
Lakeland, Florida 33802
B, T, D

University of Florida
Ornamental Horticulture Dept.
Gainesville, Florida 32601
B, M, P

Georgia

University of Georgia
Department of Horticulture
Athens, Georgia 30601
B, M, P, T, D

Hawaii

University of Hawaii
Department of Horticulture
Honolulu, Hawaii 96822
B, M, P, T

Illinois

Illinois State at Normal
Department of Agriculture
Normal, Illinois 61761
M, T

Southern Illinois University
Department of Plant & Soil Science
Carbondale, Illinois 62901
B, M

University of Illinois
Department of Horticulture
Urbana, Illinois 61801
B, M, P

Indiana

Purdue University
Department of Horticulture
Lafayette, Indiana 47907
B, M, P, T, D

Iowa

Iowa State University of Science and Technology
Department of Horticulture
Ames, Iowa 50010
B, M, P, T, D

Kansas

Kansas State University
Department of Horticulture
Manhattan, Kansas 66502
B, M, P, T, C

Kentucky

Eastern Kentucky University
Department of Horticulture
Richmond, Kentucky 40475
B, AAS, T, D

Murray State University
Department of Horticulture
Murray, Kentucky 42071
B, M, AS, T, D

University of Kentucky
Lexington, Kentucky 40506
B, M, P, T, D

Louisiana

Louisiana State University and A & M University
Department of Horticulture
Baton Rouge, Louisiana 70803
B, M, P

Louisiana Tech. University
Department of Horticulture
Ruston, Louisiana 71270
B, T

McNeese State University
Department of Horticulture
Lake Charles, Louisiana 70601
B, T, D

Southeastern Louisiana University
Department of Horticulture
Hammond, Louisiana 70401
B, T, D

University of Southwestern Louisiana
Department of Horticulture
Lafayette, Louisiana 70501
B, T, D

Maine

University of Maine
Department of Plant & Soil Sciences
Orono, Maine 04473
B, M, P, AS, T, D

Maryland

University of Maryland
Department of Horticulture

College Park, Maryland 20740
B, M, P, T

Massachusetts

University of Massachusetts
Department of Horticulture
Amherst, Massachusetts 01002
B, M, P, AS, T

Michigan

Michigan State University
Institute of Agricultural Technology
Department of Horticulture
East Lansing, Michigan 48823
B, M, P, AS, T, C, D

Minnesota

University of Minnesota
Department of Horticulture
St. Paul, Minnesota 55101
B, M, P, T

Mississippi

Mississippi State University
Department of Horticulture
State College, Mississippi 39762
B, M, P, T

Missouri

Lincoln University
Department of Horticulture
Jefferson City, Missouri 65101
B, T

Northwest Missouri State University
Department of Horticulture
Maryville, Missouri 64468
B, T, D

Southwest Missouri State University
Department of Horticulture
Springfield, Missouri 65802
B, T, D

University of Missouri
Department of Horticulture
Columbia, Missouri 65201
B, M, P, T, D

Montana

Montana State University
Department of Horticulture
Bozeman, Montana 59715
B, M, P, T, D

Nebraska

University of Nebraska
Department of Horticulture
Lincoln, Nebraska 68503
B, M, P, T, N

Nevada

University of Nevada
Max C. Fleischmann College of Agriculture
9th and Valley Road
Reno, Nevada 89507
B, M, AS, T, N, C, D

New Hampshire

University of New Hampshire
Department of Horticulture
Durham, New Hampshire 03824
B, M, P, AAS, T

New Jersey

Rutgers—The State University
Department of Horticulture
New Brunswick, New Jersey 08903
B, M, P, T, D

New Mexico

New Mexico State University
Department of Horticulture
Las Cruces, New Mexico 88003
B, M, AS, T, D

New York

Cornell University
Department of Floriculture & Ornamental Horticulture
Ithaca, New York 14850
B, M, P, T, D

North Carolina

North Carolina Agricultural & Technical University
Department of Horticulture
Greensboro, North Carolina 27411
B

North Carolina State University
Department of Horticulture

Raleigh, North Carolina 27607
B, M, P, T, D

North Dakota

North Dakota State University
Department of Horticulture
Fargo, North Dakota 58102
B, M, AS, T, N, C, D

Ohio

Ohio State University
Department of Horticulture
Columbus, Ohio 43210
B, M, P, T, D

Oklahoma

Oklahoma State University
Department of Horticulture
Stillwater, Oklahoma 74074
B

Oregon

Oregon State University
Department of Horticulture
Corvallis, Oregon 97331
B, M, P, T, D

Pennsylvania

Delaware Valley College of Science and Agriculture
Department of Horticulture
Doylestown, Pennsylvania 18901
B, T, D

Pennsylvania State University
Department of Horticulture
103 Tyson Bldg.
University Park, Pennsylvania 16802
B, M, P, N, C, D

Puerto Rico

University of Puerto Rico
Department of Horticulture
College Station
Mayaguez, Puerto Rico 00708
B, M, T, C, D

Rhode Island

University of Rhode Island
Plant and Soil Science Dept.
Woodward Hall
Kingston, Rhode Island 02881
B, M, P, T, D

South Carolina

Clemson University
Department of Horticulture
Clemson, South Carolina 29631
B, M, P, T, D

South Dakota

South Dakota State University
Department of Horticulture
Brookings, South Dakota 57006
B, T, D

Tennessee

Middle Tennessee State University
Department of Horticulture
Murfreesboro, Tennessee 37130
B

Texas

Sam Houston State University
Department of Horticulture
Huntsville, Texas 77340
B, M, T, D

Texas A & I University
Department of Horticulture
Kingsville, Texas 87363
B, AAS, AS, T

Texas A & M University
Department of Horticulture
College Station, Texas 77843
B, M, P, T

Texas State Technical Institute
James Connally Campus
Department of Horticulture
Waco, Texas 76705
B, AS, T, C

Texas Tech University
Department of Horticulture
Lubbock, Texas 79409
B, M

Utah

Brigham Young University
Department of Horticulture
Provo, Utah 84601
B, M, T, D

Utah State University
Extension Services
Department of Horticulture
Independent Street
Logan, Utah 84321
B, M, P, AAS, T, C, D

Vermont

University of Vermont
Department of Horticulture
Burlington, Vermont 05401
B, M, P, T, D

Virginia

Virginia Polytechnic Institute and State University
Blacksburg, Virginia 24061
B, M, P, WS, T, D

Washington

Washington State University
Department of Horticulture
Pullman, Washington 99163
B, M, P, T, D

Wisconsin

University of Wisconsin
Department of Horticulture

Madison, Wisconsin 53706
B, M, P, T

Canada

Laval University
Plant Science Department
St. Foy
Quebec City, Canada
B, M, AAS, T, C

University of Alberta
Horticulture Division
Department of Plant Science
Edmonton, Canada
B, M, D

University of British Columbia
Department of Plant Science
Vancouver 8, B.C., Canada
B, M, P, T

University of Guelph
Horticultural Science Dept.
Ontario, Canada
B, M, P, T, D

University of Manitoba
Department of Plant Science
Winnipeg, Manitoba, Canada R3T 2N2
B, M, P, T, D

University of Saskatchewan
Department of Horticulture
Saskatoon, Canada
B, M, T